COMBINED
Sound of Living Waters
and Fresh Sounds
Words only edition

GW00361743

SLW

COMBINED
Sound of Living Waters
and Fresh Sounds
Words only edition

compiled by
BETTY PULKINGHAM
and
JEANNE HARPER

HODDER AND STOUGHTON
LONDON SYDNEY AUCKLAND TORONTO

Printed in Great Britain for Hodder and Stoughton Limited, Mill Road,
Dunton Green, Sevenoaks, Kent, by Hunt Barnard Printing Ltd,
Aylesbury, Bucks.

CONTENTS

FOREWORD

We are now happy to present a combined *Sound of Living Waters* and *Fresh Sounds* wordbook for the convenience of singing groups and congregations who have access to both music editions. There is a wealth of material here for the forward-looking Church: for those who want to find a happy blending of the old and new in their worship life; for youth workers and those who teach children; for those who would press on past the gates of musical purism or those of "innovation at any cost" and seek a broad base for their corporate song offering.

We proudly offer this book as a manual of praise. It is designed for Christians who cannot help themselves, who simply *must* rejoice!

Sound of Living Waters

Songs of Renewal

SOUND OF LIVING WATERS

CONTENTS

1.

Alleluia No. 1

Don Fishel

Refrain
Alleluia, alleluia, give thanks to the risen Lord,
Alleluia, alleluia, give praise to his name.

1. Jesus is Lord of all the earth.
   He is the King of creation.

2. Spread the good news o'er all the earth.
   Jesus has died and has risen.

3. We have been crucified with Christ.
   Now we shall live for ever.

4. God has proclaimed the just reward,
   Life for all men, alleluia.

5. Come let us praise the living God,
   Joyfully sing to our Saviour.

2.

The canticle of the gift

Pat Uhl Howard

Refrain
O what a gift! What a wonderful gift!
Who can tell the wonders of the Lord?
Let us open our eyes, our ears, and our hearts;
It is Christ the Lord, it is he!

1. In the stillness of the night
   When the world was asleep,
   The almighty Word leapt out.
   He came to Mary, he came to us,
   Christ came to the land of Galilee.
       Christ our Lord and our King!

2. On the night before he died
   It was Passover night,
   And he gathered his friends together.
   He broke the bread, he blessed the wine;
   It was the gift of his love and his life.
       Christ our Lord and our King!

3. On the hill of Calvary
   The world held its breath,
   For there for the world to see,
   God gave his Son, his very own Son
   For the love of you and me.
       Christ our Lord and our King!

4. Early on that morning
   When the guards were sleeping,
   Back to life came he!
   He conquered death, he conquered sin,
   But the vict'ry he gave to you and me!
       Christ our Lord and our King!

5. Some day with the saints
   We will come before our Father
   And then we will shout and dance and sing.
   For in our midst for our eyes to see
   Will be Christ our Lord and our King!
       Christ our Lord and our King!

3. Something in my heart

Anon.

Something in my heart like a stream running free
Makes me feel so happy, as happy as can be;
When I think of Jesus and what he's done for me,
Something in my heart like a stream running free.

4. Give me oil in my lamp

Anon.

1. Give me oil in my lamp, keep me burning.
   Give me oil in my lamp, I pray.
   Give me oil in my lamp, keep me burning,
   Keep me burning 'til the break of day.

Refrain
Sing hosanna, sing hosanna,
Sing hosanna to the King of kings!

2. Make me a fisher of men, keep me seeking...

3. Give me joy in my heart, keep me singing...

4. Give me love in my heart, keep me serving...

5. Amazing grace

John Newton

1. Amazing grace! How sweet the sound
   That saved a wretch like me.
   I once was lost, but now am found,
   Was blind, but now I see.

2. 'Twas grace that taught my heart to fear,
    And grace my fears relieved.
How precious did that grace appear
    The hour I first believed.

3. Through many dangers, toils and snares,
    I have already come;
    'Tis grace hath brought me safe thus far,
    And grace will lead me home.

4. When we've been there ten thousand years.
    Bright shining as the sun,
We've no less days to sing God's praise
    Than when we've first begun.

6.   Oh! How good is the Lord

Anon.

Refrain
Oh! Oh! Oh! how good is the Lord. *Three times*
I never will forget what he has done for me.

1. He gives me salvation, how good is the Lord.
                                Three times
    I never will forget what he has done for me.

2. He gives me his blessings...

3. He gives me his Spirit...

4. He gives me his healing...

5. He gives me his glory...

7.   I will sing, I will sing

Max Dyer

I will sing, I will sing a song unto the Lord. *Three times*
Alleluia, glory to the Lord.

Refrain
Allelu, alleluia, glory to the Lord. *Three times*
Alleluia, glory to the Lord.

Optional verses:

We will come, we will come as one before the Lord.
  Alleluia, glory to the Lord.

If the Son, if the Son shall make you free,
  You shall be free indeed.

They that sow in tears shall reap in joy.
  Alleluia, glory to the Lord.

Every knee shall bow and every tongue confess
  That Jesus Christ is Lord.

In his name, in his name we have the victory.
  Alleluia, glory to the Lord.

8.

Let us give thanks

Brian Howard

Refrain
Let us give thanks
That our names are written,
Let us give thanks
That our names are written,
Written in the book of life,
Inscribed upon his palms,
Written in the book of life,
Inscribed upon his palms.

1. Rejoice not that devils flee in his name.
    Rejoice not in the power that he gave;
    For he came to break the bonds of sin.
    Yes he did, he came to set us free, so freely we sing.

2. For he came to give us life,
    That we might have it more abundantly;
    Came to break the power of sin, he did.
    Yes, he did, he came to set us free, so freely we sing.

3. Let us give thanks,
    Thanks unto the Father,
    Thanks unto the Son
    Thanks to the Holy Spirit,
    Our Lord God Three in One.

9.

Morning has broken

Eleanor Farjeon

1. Morning has broken like the first morning;
    Blackbird has spoken like the first bird.
    Praise for the singing! Praise for the morning!
    Praise for them springing fresh from the word.

2. Sweet the rain's new fall, sunlit from heaven,
   Like the first dew fall on the first grass.
   Praise for the sweetness of the wet garden,
   Sprung in completeness where his feet pass.

3. Mine is the sunlight! Mine is the morning;
   Born of the one light Eden saw play.
   Praise with elation! Praise every morning
   God's re-creation of the new day.

10.   Rejoice in the Lord always

Anon.

Rejoice in the Lord always, and again I say rejoice.
Rejoice in the Lord always, and again I say rejoice.
Rejoice, rejoice, and again I say rejoice.
Rejoice, rejoice, and again I say rejoice.

11.   Praise to the Lord

Joachim Neander

1. Praise to the Lord, the almighty, the King of creation;
   O my soul, praise him for he is thy health and salvation;
   Join the great throng,
   Psaltery, organ and song,
   Sounding in glad adoration.

2. Praise to the Lord, over all things he gloriously reigneth;
   Borne as on eagle wings, safely his saints he sustaineth.
   Hast thou not seen
   How all thou needest hath been
   Granted in what he ordaineth?

3. Praise to the Lord, who doth prosper thy way and defend
thee;
  Surely his goodness and mercy shall ever attend thee;
    Ponder anew
    What the almighty can do,
Who with his love doth befriend thee.

4. Praise to the Lord! O let all that is in me adore him!
  All that hath breath join with Abraham's seed to adore
him!

    Let the "Amen"
    Sum all our praises again
Now as we worship before him.

12.   Angel voices ever singing

Francis Pott

1.   Angel voices ever singing
    Round thy throne of light,
  Angel harps for ever ringing,
    Rest not day nor night;
  Thousands only live to bless thee,
  And confess thee
    Lord of might.

2.   Thou who art beyond the farthest
    Mortal eye can scan.
  Can it be that thou regardest
    Songs of sinful man?
  Can we know that thou art near us
  And wilt hear us?
    Yes, we can.

3. Yes, we know that thou rejoicest
   O'er each work of thine;
Thou didst ears and hands and voices
   For the praise design;
Craftsman's art and music's measure
For thy pleasure
   All combine.

4. In thy house, great God, we offer
   Of thine own to thee;
And for thine acceptance proffer
   All unworthily,
Hearts and minds and hands and voices
In our choicest
   Psalmody.

5. Honour, glory, might, and merit
   Thine shall ever be,
Father, Son, and Holy Spirit,
   Blessed Trinity.
Of the best that thou hast given
Earth and heaven
   Render thee.

13.   This is the day

Anon.

1. This is the day, this is the day
   That the Lord has made, that the Lord has made.
We will rejoice, we will rejoice
   and be glad in it, and be glad in it.

This is the day that the Lord has made.
We will rejoice and be glad in it.

This is the day that the Lord has made.

2. This is the day when he rose again.

3. This is the day when the Spirit came.

14. Praise him

Anon.

1. Praise him, praise him,
   Praise him in the morning,
   Praise him in the noontime,
   Praise him, praise him,
   Praise him when the sun goes down.

2. Jesus.	4. Trust him.
3. Love him.	5. Serve him.

15. Hallelujah! Jesus is Lord!

Mimi Armstrong Farra
Adapted from Rev. 7

Refrain
Hallelujah! Hallelujah! Hallelujah! Jesus is Lord!
Hallelujah! Hallelujah! Hallelujah! Jesus is King!

1. All gather round the throne of the Lamb,
   His praises sing throughout eternity.

2. Lift up your voice with the thousands who cry:
   "Worthy, worthy art thou, Lamb of God."

3. Blessing and honour and glory and pow'r
   Be unto him for ever and ever.

4. All glory be to the one Triune God,
   The Father, Son, and the – Holy Spirit.

16.   **Jesus Christ is alive today**

Anon.

Jesus Christ is alive today
[$_{we}^{I}$] know, [$_{we}^{I}$] know it's true.
Sovereign of the universe,
[$_{We}^{I}$] give him homage due.
Seated there at God's right hand,
[$_{We\ are}^{I\ am}$] with him in the promised land.

Jesus lives and reigns in [$_{you.}^{me.}$]
That's how I know it's true.

17.   **O for a thousand tongues**

Charles Wesley

1. O for a thousand tongues to sing
   My great redeemer's praise,
   The glories of my God and King,
   The triumphs of his grace.

2. Jesus! the name that charms our fears,
   That bids our sorrows cease;
   'Tis music in the sinner's ears,
   'Tis life, and health, and peace.

3. He breaks the power of cancelled sin,
   He sets the prisoner free;
   His blood can make the foulest clean,
   His blood availed for me.

4. He speaks, and listening to his voice,
   New life the dead receive,
   The mournful, broken hearts rejoice,
   The humble poor believe.

5. Hear him, ye deaf; his praise, ye dumb,
   Your loosened tongues employ;
   Ye blind, behold your Saviour come,
   And leap, ye lame, for joy!

6. My gracious master and my God
   Assist me to proclaim,
   To spread through all the earth abroad
   The honours of thy name.

18. Thank you, thank you, Jesus

Anon.

1. Thank you, thank you, Jesus.
   Thank you, thank, you, Jesus.
   Thank you, thank you, Jesus, in my heart.
   Thank you, thank you, Jesus.
   Oh, thank you, thank you, Jesus.
   Thank you, thank you, Jesus, in my heart.

2. You can't make me doubt him.
   You can't make me doubt him in my heart.
   You can't make me doubt him,
   I know too much about him.
   Thank you, thank you, Jesus, in my heart.

3. I can't live without him.
   I can't live without him in my heart.
   I can't live without him,
   I know too much about him.
   Thank you, thank you, Jesus, in my heart.

4. Glory, hallelujah!
    Glory, hallelujah, in my heart!
    Glory, hallelujah!
    Glory, hallelujah!
    Thank you, thank you, Jesus, in my heart!

19.   Holy, holy

Jimmy Owens

1. Holy, holy, holy, holy.
    Holy, holy, Lord God Almighty;
    And we lift our hearts before you as a token of our love,
      Holy, holy, holy, holy.

2. Gracious Father, gracious Father,
    We're so glad to be your children, gracious Father;
    And we lift our heads before you as a token of our love,
      Gracious Father, gracious Father.

3. Precious Jesus, precious Jesus,
    We're so glad that you've redeemed us, precious Jesus,
    And we lift our hands before you as a token of our love,
      Precious Jesus, precious Jesus.

4. Holy Spirit, Holy Spirit,
    Come and fill our hearts anew, Holy Spirit,
    And we lift our voice before you as a token of our love,
      Holy Spirit, Holy Spirit.

5. *Repeat verse 1.*

6. Hallelujah, hallelujah, hallelujah, hallelujah,
    And we lift our hearts before you as a token of our love.
      Hallelujah, hallelujah.

20. Let all that is within me

Anon.

Let all that is within me cry, "Holy."
Let all that is within me cry, "Holy."
Holy, holy, holy is the Lamb that was slain.

Let all that is within me cry, "Worthy"...
"Jesus"...
"Glory"...

21. Son of God

Oressa Wise

1. Son of God, Son of God,
    We come before you
    To love and adore you,
    Son of God.

2. Word of God, Word of God,
    We come to hear you,
    To always be near you,
    Word of God.

3. Lamb of God, Lamb of God,
    We come to bless you,
    To ever confess you,
    Lamb of God.

4. *Repeat verse 1.*

22.

God himself is with us

Gerhardt Tersteegen

1. God himself is with us;
    Let us all adore him,
   And with awe appear before him.
   God is here within us:
    Soul in silence fear him,
   Humbly, fervently draw near him.
    Now his own who have known
   God, in worship lowly,
    Yield their spirits wholly.

2. Come, abide within me;
    Let my soul, like Mary,
   Be thine earthly sanctuary.
   Come, indwelling Spirit,
    With transfigured splendour;
   Love and honour will I render,
    Where I go here below,
   Let me bow before thee,
    Know thee, and adore thee.

3. Gladly we surrender
    Earth's deceitful treasures,
   Pride of life, and sinful pleasures:
   Gladly, Lord, we offer
    Thine to be for ever,
   Soul and life and each endeavour,
    Thou alone shalt be known
   Lord of all our being,
    Life's true way decreeing.

23.   We see the Lord

Anon.

We see the Lord,
We see the Lord,
And he is high and lifted up,
And his train fills the temple.
He is high and lifted up,
And his train fills the temple.
The angels cry, "Holy",
The angels cry, "Holy",
The angels cry, "Holy is the Lord."

24.   He is Lord

Anon.

He is Lord, he is Lord,
He is risen from the dead, and he is Lord.
Every knee shall bow,
Every tongue confess
That Jesus Christ is Lord.

25.   Alleluia

Anon.

1. Alleluia. *Eight times*

2. How I love him.

3. Blessed Jesus.

4. My Redeemer

5. Jesus is Lord.

6. Alleluia.

26. Father we adore you
(3-part round)

Terrye Coelho

Father, we adore you;
Lay our lives before you.
How we love you.

Jesus we adore you...

Spirit we adore you...

27. Thank you, thank you, Jesus

Anon.

1. Thank you, thank you, Jesus.
   Thank you, thank you, Jesus.
   Oh, thank you, thank you, Jesus in my heart.
   Thank you, thank you, Jesus.
   Oh, thank you, thank you, Jesus.
   Oh, thank you, thank you, Jesus, in my heart.

2. Love you, love you, Jesus.
   Love you, love you, Jesus.
   Oh, love you, love you, Jesus in my heart...

3. Father, God almighty.
   Father, God almighty,
   Oh, Father, God almighty, take my heart...

4. Glory hallelujah!
   Glory hallelujah!
   Oh, glory hallelujah in my heart...

28.   **Thou art worthy**

Pauline Michael Mills
and Tom Smail. Adapted from
Rev 4:11 and 5:9.10

1. Thou art worthy, thou art worthy,
      Thou art worthy, O Lord.
   Thou art worthy to receive glory,
      Glory and honour and power.
   For thou hast created, hast all things created,
      For thou hast created all things.
   And for thy pleasure they are created;
      Thou art worthy, O Lord.

2. Thou art worthy, thou art worthy,
      Thou art worthy, O Lamb.
   Thou art worthy to receive glory,
      And power at the Father's right hand.
   For thou hast redeemed us, hast ransomed and cleaned us
      By thy blood setting us free;
   In white robes arrayed us, kings and priests made us,
      And we are reigning in thee.

29.   **Spirit of the living God**

Daniel Iverson

Spirit of the living God, fall afresh on me.
Spirit of the living God, fall afresh on me.
Break me, melt me, mould me, fill me.
Spirit of the living God, fall afresh on me.

30. Jesus, never have I heard a name

Anon.

Jesus, Jesus, Jesus,
Never have I heard a name that thrills my soul like thine.

Jesus, Jesus, Jesus,
Oh what matchless grace that links that precious name with
    mine.

31.

This song is omitted for copyright reasons

32. Jesus, Jesus, wonderful Lord

Sylvia Lawton

1. Jesus, Jesus, wonderful Lord,
   Gently you touched me and made my life whole;
   How can I thank you except that I see
   Your way of life is truly for me?

2. Jesus, Jesus, take my life,
   Jesus, Jesus, I give to you
   All things, always yours to become.
   Jesus my Saviour, I will be thine.

3. Seeing, looking with new eyes;
   Loving, caring just as you do;
   Learning all things from your point of view;
   Lord Jesus Christ, your touch is so true.

33. Spirit divine

Andrew Reed

1. Spirit divine, attend our prayers,
     And make this house thy home;
   Descend with all thy gracious powers,
     O come, great Spirit, come!

2. Come as the light; to us reveal
     Our emptiness and woe,
   And lead us in those paths of life
     Whereon the righteous go.

3. Come as the fire, and purge our hearts
     Like sacrificial flame;
   Let our whole soul an offering be
     To our redeemer's name.

4. Come as the dove, and spread thy wings,
     The wings of peaceful love;
   And let thy Church on earth become
     Blest as the Church above.

5. Spirit divine, attend our prayers;
     Make a lost world thy home;
   Descend with all thy gracious powers;
     O come, great Spirit, come!

34. I want to walk as a child of the light

Kathleen Thomerson

1. I want to walk as a child of the light.
   I want to follow Jesus.
   God set the stars to give light to the world.
   The star of my life is Jesus.

Refrain

In him there is no darkness at all,
   The night and the day are both alike.
The Lamb is the light of the city of God.
   Shine in my heart, Lord Jesus.

2.   I want to see the brightness of God.
   I want to look at Jesus.
   Clear sun of righteousness, shine on my path,
   And show me the way to the Father.

3.   I'm looking for the coming of Christ.
   I want to be with Jesus.
   When we have run with patience the race,
   We shall know the joy of Jesus.

35.   In Christ there is no east or west

John Oxenham

1.   In Christ there is no east or west,
    In him no south or north,
  But one great fellowship of love
    Throughout the whole wide earth.

2.   In him shall true hearts everywhere
    Their high communion find;
  His service is the golden cord
    Close binding all mankind.

3.   Join hands then, brothers of the faith,
    Whate'er your race may be;
  Who serves my Father as a son
    Is surely kin to me.

4. In Christ now meet both east and west,
      In him meet south and north.
    All Christly souls are one in him
      Throughout the whole wide earth.

36. Lord, I want to be a Christian
American folk hymn

1. Lord, I want to be a Christian,
      In-a my heart, in-a my heart.
    Lord, I want to be a Christian,
      In-a my heart.
    In-a my heart, in-a my heart,
    Lord, I want to be a Christian in-a my heart.

2. Lord, I want to be more loving...

3. Lord, I want to be like Jesus...

4. Lord, I want to praise you freely...

37. Day by day
Richard of Chichester
and Jeanne Harper

1. Day by day, dear Lord, of thee three things I pray:
    To see thee more clearly,
    To love thee more dearly,
    To follow thee more nearly day by day.

SOUND OF LIVING WATERS

2. Day by day, dear Lord, of thee three things I pray:
   To trust thee more fully,
   To leave things more wholly,
   To lean on thee securely day by day.

38. **Day by day**

Richard of Chichester

   Day by day,
   O dear Lord, three things I pray:
     To see thee more clearly,
     Love thee more dearly,
     Follow thee more nearly,
   Day by day.

39. **Reach out and touch the Lord**

Bill Harmon

Reach out and touch the Lord as he goes by.
You'll find he's not too busy to hear your heart's cry.
He's passing by this moment your needs to supply.
Reach out and touch the Lord as he goes by.

40. **I want to live for Jesus every day**

Anon.

1. I want to live for Jesus every day.
   I want to live for Jesus, come what may.
   Take the world and all its pleasure,
   I've got a more enduring treasure.
   I want to live for Jesus every day.

2. I'm gonna' live for Jesus every day...

41.　He shall teach you all things

He shall teach you all things,
　He shall teach you all things,
And bring all things to your remembrance,
　And bring all things to your remembrance.

42.　Kum ba yah
("Come by here")

Traditional
spiritual

1.　Kum ba yah, my Lord, Kum ba yah,
　　Kum ba yah, my Lord, Kum ba yah;
　　Kum ba yah, my Lord, Kum ba yah,
　　　O Lord, Kum ba yah.

2.　Someone's crying, Lord, Kum ba yah...

3.　Someone's singing, Lord, Kum ba yah...

4.　Someone's praying, Lord, Kum ba yah...

43.　O Breath of Life
Bessie Porter Head

1.　O Breath of Life, come sweeping through us,
　　Revive thy Church with life and power.
　　O Breath of Life, come, cleanse, renew us,
　　And fit thy Church to meet this hour.

2. O Wind of God, come bend us, break us,
   Till humbly we confess our need:
Then in thy tenderness re-make us,
   Revive, restore; for this we plead.

3. O Breath of Love, come breathe within us,
   Renewing thought and will and heart;
Come, love of Christ, afresh to win us,
   Revive thy Church in every part.

4. Revive us, Lord! Is zeal abating
   While harvest fields are vast and white?
Revive us, Lord, the world is waiting,
   Equip thy Church to spread the light.

44.　　　Lord of all hopefulness

Jan Struther

1. Lord of all hopefulness, Lord of all joy,
   Whose trust, ever childlike, no cares could destroy,
   Be there at our waking, and give us, we pray,
   Your bliss in our hearts, Lord, at the break of the day.

2. Lord of all eagerness, Lord of all faith,
   Whose strong hands were skilled at the plane and the
                                          lathe,
   Be there at our labours, and give us, we pray,
   Your strength in our hearts, Lord, at the noon of the day.

3. Lord of all kindliness, Lord of all grace,
   Your hands swift to welcome, your arms to embrace,
   Be there at our homing, and give us, we pray,
   Your love in our hearts, Lord, at the eve of the day.

4. Lord of all gentleness, Lord of all calm,
    Whose voice is contentment, whose presence is balm,
    Be there at our sleeping, and give us, we pray,
    Your peace in our hearts, Lord, at the end of the day.

45. & 46. At the name of Jesus

Caroline M. Noel

1. At the name of Jesus
        Every knee shall bow,
    Every tongue confess him
        King of glory now.
    'Tis the Father's pleasure
        We should call him Lord,
    Who from the beginning
        Was the mighty Word.

2. Humbled for a season,
        To receive a name
    From the lips of sinners,
        Unto whom he came,
    Faithfully he bore it,
        Spotless to the last,
    Brought it back victorious,
        When from death he passed.

3. Bore it up triumphant,
        With its human light,
    Through all ranks of creatures,
        To the central height,
    To the throne of Godhead,
        To the Father's breast;
    Filled it with the glory
        Of that perfect rest.

4. In your hearts enthrone him,
   There let him subdue
All that is not holy,
   All that is not true:
Crown him as your captain
   In temptation's hour;
Let his will enfold you
   In its light and power.

5. Brothers, this Lord Jesus
   Shall return again,
With his Father's glory
   O'er the earth to reign;
For all wreaths of empire
   Meet upon his brow,
And our hearts confess him
   King of glory now.

47. I want to walk with Jesus Christ

St. Paul's Erith
1964 House Party

1. I want to walk with Jesus Christ,
   All the days I live of this life on earth,
To give to him complete control
   Of body and of soul.

Refrain
Follow him, follow him, yield your life to him,
   He has conquered death, he is King of kings.
Accept the joy which he gives to those
   Who yield their lives to him.

2. I want to learn to speak to him,
   To pray to him, confess my sin,
   To open my life and let him in,
   For joy will then be mine.

3. I want to learn to speak of him,
   My life must show that he lives in me.
   My deeds, my thoughts, my words must speak
   All of his love for me.

4. I want to learn to read his word,
   For this is how I know the way
   To live my life as pleases him,
   In holiness and joy.

5. O Holy Spirit of the Lord,
   Enter now into this heart of mine,
   Take full control of my selfish will
   And make me wholly thine.

48. How sweet the name of Jesus sounds
John Newton

1. How sweet the name of Jesus sounds
   In a believer's ear!
   It soothes his sorrows, heals his wounds,
   And drives away his fear.

2. It makes the wounded spirit whole,
   And calms the troubled breast;
   'Tis manna to the hungry soul,
   And to the weary rest.

3. Dear name, the rock on which I build,
   My shield and hiding place,
   My never-failing treasury, filled
   With boundless stores of grace.

4. Jesus! My Shepherd, Brother, Friend,
   My Prophet, Priest, and King,
   My Lord, my life, my way, my end,
   Accept the praise I bring.

5. Weak is the effort of my heart,
   And cold my warmest thought;
   But when I see thee as thou art,
   I'll praise thee as I ought.

6. Till then I would thy love proclaim
   With every fleeting breath;
   And may the music of thy name
   Refresh my soul in death.

49.   Here comes Jesus

Anon.

Here comes Jesus, see him walking on the water,
   He'll lift you up and he'll help you to stand.
Here comes Jesus, he's the master of the waves that roll.
   Here comes Jesus, he'll make you whole.

*Repeat in ascending keys, ending with the following (extra)
words:*

Here comes Jesus, he'll save your soul.

50. Silver and gold have I none

Anon.

Verse
Peter and John went to pray,
  they met a lame man on the way.
He asked for alms and held out his palms,
  and this is what Peter did say:

Refrain
"Silver and gold have I none,
  but such as I have give I thee.
In the name of Jesus Christ
  of Nazareth, rise up and walk!"

He went walking and leaping and praising God,
  walking and leaping and praising God.
"In the name of Jesus Christ
  of Nazareth, rise up and walk."

51. There is a balm in Gilead

North American spiritual

Refrain
There is a balm in Gilead
  to make the wounded whole.
There is a balm in Gilead
  to heal the sin-sick soul.

1. Sometimes I feel discouraged,
      and think my work's in vain,
    but then the Holy Spirit
      revives my soul again.

2. If you cannot sing like angels,
   if you cannot preach like Paul,
   you can tell the love of Jesus
   and say he died for all.

52. Dear Lord and Father

John Greenleaf Whittier

1. Dear Lord and Father of mankind,
   Forgive our foolish ways!
   Reclothe us in our rightful mind:
   In purer lives thy service find,
   In deeper rev'rance praise.

2. In simple trust like theirs who heard,
   Beside the Syrian sea,
   The gracious calling of the Lord,
   Let us like them, without a word,
   Rise up and follow thee.

3. O sabbath rest by Galilee!
   O calm of hills above,
   Where Jesus knelt to share with thee
   The silence of eternity,
   Interpreted by love.

4. With that deep hush subduing all
   Our words and works that drown
   The tender whisper of thy call,
   As noiseless let thy blessing fall
   As fell thy manna down.

5. Drop thy still dews of quietness
   Till all our strivings cease:
   Take from our souls the strain and stress,
   And let our ordered lives confess
   The beauty of thy peace.

6. Breathe through the heats of our desire
    Thy coolness and thy balm;
  Let sense be dumb, let flesh retire;
    Speak through the earthquake, wind and fire,
  O still small voice of calm.

53.   The bell song

David Lynch

1. You gotta have love in your heart.
   You gotta have love in your heart.
   You knew it was Jesus right from the start
   You gotta have love in your heart.

2. You gotta have peace on your mind.
   You knew it was Jesus there all the time.

3. You gotta have joy in your soul.
   The love of Jesus will make you whole.

4. La la la la...

54.   By your stripes

Pamela Greenwood

By your stripes, Lord, I'm healed, hallelujah!
In your word it is revealed, hallelujah!
Yes, you bore it all for me, on the cross of Calvary
So that now I can go free, hallelujah!

55. ## Alleluia! sing to Jesus

William Dix

1. Alleluia! Sing to Jesus!
    His the sceptre, his the throne;
   Alleluia! His the triumph,
    His the victory alone;
   Hark! The songs of peaceful Zion
    Thunder like a mighty flood;
   Jesus out of every nation
    Hath redeemed us by his blood.

2. Alleluia! Not as orphans
    Are we left in sorrow now;
   Alleluia! He is near us,
    Faith believes, nor questions how:
   Though the cloud from sight received him,
    When the forty days were o'er,
   Shall our hearts forget his promise,
    'I am with you evermore'?

3. Alleluia! Bread of heaven,
    Thou on earth our food, our stay!
   Alleluia! Here the sinful
    Flee to thee from day to day:
   Intercessor, friend of sinners,
    Earth's redeemer, plead for me,
   Where the songs of all the sinless
    Sweep across the crystal sea.

4. Alleluia! King eternal,
    Thee the Lord of lords we own:
   Alleluia! Born of Mary,
    Earth thy footstool, heav'n thy throne
   Thou within the veil hast entered,
    Robed in flesh, our great high priest
   Thou on earth both priest and victim
    In the eucharistic feast.

5. Alleluia! Sing to Jesus!
    His the sceptre, his the throne;
   Alleluia! His the triumph,
    His the victory alone;
   Hark! the songs of holy Zion
    Thunder like a mighty flood;
   Jesus out of every nation
    Hath redeemed us by his blood.

56. Blow, thou cleansing wind
Alan Teage

1. Blow, thou cleansing wind from heaven,
    Burn, thou fire, within our hearts.
   Spirit of the Lord, possess us,
    Fill our lives in every part.
   Mind of Christ, be thou our ruler.
    Word of truth, be thou our guide;
   Leave no part of us unhallowed.
    Come, O come in us abide.

2. Fill thy Church, inspire and strengthen,
    Chasten, mould, empower and lead.
   Make us one, and make us joyful,
    Give us grace for every need.
   Be our life, build firm thy kingdom.
    Be our strength, who are but frail.
   Then indeed against us never
    Shall the gates of hell prevail.

3. Win the world! Baptize the nations!
      Open every blinded eye.
   Leave no sinner unconvicted;
      Leave no soul untouched and dry.
   Conquering love, take thou the kingdom,
      Rule thou over all our days;
   Then in glory and rejoicing
      Earth shall echo with thy praise.

57.   Jesus

Debby Kerner

1. Jesus. *Five times*   4. He lives.
2. He died.   5. We live through him.
3. He rose.   6. Jesus.

58.   Seek ye first
                    (2-part round)

Karen Lafferty

Seek ye first the kingdom of God,
   And his righteousness,
And all these things shall be added unto you;
   Allelu, alleluia.

Alleluia, alleluia, alleluia,
   Allelu, alleluia.

59. Fear not! rejoice and be glad

Priscilla Wright
Adapted from Joel 2:21-27

Refrain
Fear not, rejoice and be glad,
The Lord hath done a great thing;
Hath poured out his Spirit on all mankind
On those who confess his name.

1. The fig tree is budding, the vine beareth fruit,
     The wheat fields are golden with grain,
   Thrust in the sickle, the harvest is ripe,
     The Lord has given us rain.

2. Ye shall eat in plenty and be satisfied,
     The mountains will drip with sweet wine,
   My children shall drink of the fountain of life,
     My children will know they are mine.

3. My people shall know that I am the Lord,
     Their shame I have taken away.
   My Spirit will lead them together again,
     My Spirit will show them the way.

4. My children shall dwell in a body of love,
     A light to the world they will be:
   Life shall come forth from the Father above,
     My body will set mankind free.

60.   God is building a house

Anon.
Verses 2.3.4 Hong Sit

1. God is building a house, God is building a house,
        God is building a house that will stand.
    He is building by his plan
        With the lively stones of man,
    God is building a house that will stand.

2. God is building a house, God is building a house,
        God is building a house that will stand.
    With apostles, prophets, pastors,
        With evangelists and teachers,
    God is building a house that will stand.

3. Christ is head of this house, Christ is head of this house,
        Christ is head of this house that will stand.
    He abideth in its praise.
        Will perfect it in its ways,
    Christ is head of this house that will stand.

4. We are part of this house, we are part of this house,
        We are part of this house that will stand.
    We are called from every nation
        To enjoy his full salvation,
    We are part of this house that will stand.

61.   The kingdom of God

Brian Howard

1. The kingdom of God is neither lo here, nor lo there,
        No, the kingdom is among us.

2. The victory of God is neither lo here, nor lo there,
    No, the victory is among us.

3. The power of God is neither lo here, nor lo there,
    No, the power is among us.

4. The Spirit of God was not lost after Pentecost,
    No, the Spirit is among us.

5. The Prince of peace has not gone away, he won't let you
                                                        stray,
    No, the Prince of peace is among us.

6. The joy of the Lord is like a singing lark, deep within
                                                    your heart,
    Let it flow so freely among us.

62.

This song is omitted for copyright reasons

63.   I am the bread of life

1. I am the bread of life;
    He who/ comes to me shall not hunger;
    He who be/lieves in me shall not thirst.
    No-one can come to me
    Un/ less the Father draw him.

    Refrain
    And I will raise him up *Repeat*
    And I will raise him up on the last day.

2. The bread that I will give
    Is my/ flesh for the life of the world
    And he who/ eats of this bread,
    He shall live for ever.

3. Un/ less you eat
   Of the/ flesh of the Son of man
   And/ drink of his blood *Repeat*
   You shall/ not have life within you.

4. I am the resurrection,
   I am the life.
   He who be/ lieves in me,
   Even if he die,
   He shall live for ever.

5. Yes/ Lord, we believe
   That/ you are the Christ,
   The/ Son of God
   Who has come
   In/ to the world.

64.   ## Oh, the blood of Jesus

Anon.

1. Oh, the blood of Jesus, *Three times*
   It washes white as snow.

2. Oh, the word of Jesus,
   It cleanses white as snow.

3. Oh, the love of Jesus,
   It makes his body whole.

65. At the cross

Sankey

At the cross, at the cross where I first saw the light,
And the burden of my heart rolled away,
It was there by faith I received my sight,
And now I am happy all the day.

66. A new commandment

Anon.

A new commandment I give unto you,
   that you love one another, as I have loved you,
   that you love one another, as I have loved you.
By this shall all men know you are my disciples
   if you have love one to another.
By this shall all men know you are my disciples
   if you have love one to another.

67. God and man at table are sat down

Robert Stamps

1. O welcome, all ye noble saints of old
   As now before your very eyes unfold
   The wonders all so long ago foretold:
      God and man at table are sat down.

2. Elders, martyrs, all are falling down,
   Prophets, patriarchs are gathering round.
   What angels longed to see now man has found.
      God and man at table are sat down.

3. Who is this who spreads the victory feast?
   Who is this who makes our warring cease?
   Jesus, risen Saviour, Prince of Peace.
      God and man at table are sat down.

4. Beggars, lame and harlots also here;
   Repentant publicans are drawing near,
   Wayward sons come home without a fear,
      God and man at table are sat down.

5. Worship in the presence of the Lord
   With joyful songs and hearts in one accord,
   And let our host at table be adored.
      God and man at table are sat down.

6. When at last this earth shall pass away,
   When Jesus and his bride are one to stay,
   The feast of love is just begun that day,
      God and man at table are sat down.

68. Glory be to Jesus

Tr. Edward Caswall

1. Glory be to Jesus,
      Who in bitter pains
   Poured for me the life-blood
      From his sacred veins!

2. Grace and life eternal
      In that blood I find,
   Blest be his compassion
      Infinitely kind!

3. Blest through endless ages
      Be the precious stream
   Which from sin and sorrow
      Doth the world redeem!

4. Oft as earth exulting
        Wafts its praise on high,
    Angel-hosts rejoicing,
        Make their glad reply.

5. Lift ye then your voices;
        Swell the mighty flood;
    Louder still and louder
        Praise the precious blood.

69. We really want to thank you, Lord

Ed. Baggett

Refrain
We really want to thank you, Lord.
We really want to bless your name.
Hallelujah! Jesus is our king!

1. We thank you, Lord, for your gift to us,
        Your life so rich beyond compare,
    The gift of your body here on earth
        Of which we sing and share.

2. We thank you, Lord, for our life together,
        To live and move in the love of Christ,
    Tenderness which sets us free
        To serve you with our lives.

70. This is my commandment

Anon.

This is my commandment that you love one another,
That your joy may be full.
This is my commandment that you love one another,
That your joy may be full
That your joy may be full,
That your joy may be full;
This is my commandment that you love one another
That your joy may be full.

71. The king of love

H. W. Baker

1. The king of love my shepherd is,
    Whose goodness faileth never;
    I nothing lack if I am his,
    And he is mine for ever.

2. Where streams of living water flow,
    My ransomed soul he leadeth,
    And where the verdant pastures grow,
    With food celestial feedeth.

3. Perverse and foolish oft I strayed,
    But yet in love he sought me,
    And on his shoulder gently laid,
    And home, rejoicing, brought me.

4. In death's dark vale I fear no ill
    With thee, dear Lord, beside me;
    Thy rod and staff my comfort still,
    Thy cross before to guide me.

5. Thou spread'st a table in my sight;
    Thy unction grace bestoweth;
    And O what transport of delight
    From thy pure chalice floweth!

6. And so through all the length of days
    Thy goodness faileth never:
    Good shepherd, may I sing thy praise
    Within thy house for ever.

72. Glorious things of thee are spoken
John Newton

1. Glorious things of thee are spoken,
    Zion, city of our God.
   He whose word cannot be broken,
    Formed thee for his own abode:
   On the rock of ages founded,
    What can shake thy sure repose?
   With salvation's walls surrounded,
    Thou may'st smile at all thy foes.

2. See the streams of living waters,
    Springing from eternal love,
   Well supply thy sons and daughters,
    And all fear of want remove:
   Who can faint while such a river
    Ever flows their thirst to assuage?
   Grace which like the Lord, the giver,
    Ever flows from age to age.

3. Round each habitation hovering,
        See the cloud and fire appear!
    For a glory and a covering
        Showing that the Lord is near:
    He who gives them daily manna,
        He who listens when they cry:
    Let him hear the loud hosanna,
        Rising to his throne on high.

4. Saviour, since of Zion's city
        I through grace a member am,
    Let the world deride or pity,
        I will glory in thy name;
    Fading is the worldling's pleasure,
        All his boasted pomp and show;
    Solid joys and lasting treasure
        None but Zion's children know.

5. Blest inhabitants of Zion;
        Washed in the Redeemer's blood!
    Jesus, whom their souls rely on,
        Makes them kings and priests to God.
    'Tis his love his people raises
        Over self to reign as kings:
    And as priests, his solemn praises
        Each for a thank-offering brings.

There is no song 73

74. **God has called you**

Diane Davis

1. God has called (name), he will not fail (him,her).
   God has called (name), he will not fail (him,her).
   God has called (name), he will not fail (him,her),
   So trust in God and obey him.

2. God has called you, he will not fail you.
   So trust in God and obey him.

3. God has called us, we will not fail him.
   So trust in God and obey him.

75. **How firm a foundation**

John Rippon

1. How firm a foundation, ye saints of the Lord,
   Is laid for your faith in his excellent word!
   What more can he say than to you he hath said,
   To you that for refuge to Jesus have fled?

2. "Fear not, I am with thee; O be not dismayed!
   For I am thy God, and will still give thee aid;
   I'll strengthen thee, help thee, and cause thee to stand,
   Upheld by my righteous, omnipotent hand.

3. "When through the deep waters I call thee to go,
   The rivers of woe shall not thee overflow;
   For I will be with thee, thy troubles to bless,
   And sanctify to thee thy deepest distress.

4. "When through fiery trials thy pathway shall lie,
   My grace, all-sufficient, shall be thy supply;
   The flame shall not hurt thee; I only design
   Thy dross to consume, and thy gold to refine."

5. "The soul that to Jesus has fled for repose,
   I will not, I will not desert to his foes;
That soul, though all hell shall endeavour to shake,
   I'll never, no never, no never forsake."

76.   Complete in him

Anon.

1. The fullness of the Godhead bodily
      Dwelleth in my Lord.
   The fullness of the Godhead bodily
      Dwelleth in my Lord.
   The fullness of the Godhead bodily
      Dwelleth in my Lord
   And we are complete in him.

   Refrain
      Complete, complete,
         Complete in him,
      We are complete in him.

2. It's not by works of righteousness
      But by his grace alone...
   That we are complete in him.

3. There's nothing more that I can do
      For Jesus did it all...
   And we are complete in him.

77. The Holy Ghost Medley

Arr. Betty Pulkingham

Jesus gave her water
That was not from the well,
Gave her living water
And sent her forth to tell:
She went away singing,
And came back bringing
Others for the water
That was not from the well.

Drinking at the springs of living water,
Happy now am I, my soul is satisfied,
Drinking at the springs of living water,
What a wonderful and bounteous supply.

Spring up, O well, within my soul.
Spring up, O well, and overflow;
Spring up, O well, flow out through me.
Spring up, O well, set others free.

1. There's a river of life flowing out through me,
    It makes the lame to walk and the blind to see,
   Opens prison doors, sets the captives free,
    There's a river of life flowing out through me.

2. There's a fountain flowing from the Saviour's side,
    All my sins forgiven in that precious tide.
   Jesus paid the price when for me he died.
    There's a fountain flowing from the Saviour's side.

3. There's a risen Saviour at the Father's throne,
    Ever interceding for his very own,
   Pouring down the blessings that are his alone.
    There's a risen Saviour at the Father's throne.

4. There's a holy comforter who's sent from heaven,
    All the glorious gifts are his, and have been given,
    He'll /show us more of Jesus 'til the veil is riven.
        There's a holy comforter who's sent from heaven.

5. There's a land of rest that we may enter now,
    Freed from all our works and freed from Satan's power,
    Just /resting in the Lord each moment and each hour.
        There's a land of rest that we may enter now.

6. There's a full salvation wrought for you and me,
    From /faith to faith and /glory to glory e/ternally,
    O /Lord, just take this life and let me live for thee.
        There's a full salvation wrought for you and me.

78.   I have decided to follow Jesus

Anon.

1. I have decided to follow Jesus.
    I have decided to follow Jesus.
    I have decided to follow Jesus.
        No turning back, no turning back.

2. The world behind me, the cross before me.
        No turning back, no turning back.

3. Tho' none go with me, still I will follow.
        No turning back, no turning back.

4. Where Jesus leads me, I'll surely follow.
        No turning back, no turning back.

5. Sing glory, glory and hallelujah.
        No turning back, no turning back.

79. See the conqueror mounts in triumph

Christopher Wordsworth

1. See the conqueror mounts in triumph,
   See the King in royal state,
   Riding on the clouds, his chariot,
   To his heavenly palace gate!
       Hark! the choirs of angel voices
       Joyful alleluias sing.
       And the portals high are lifted
       To receive their heavenly King.

2. He who on the cross did suffer,
   He who from the grave arose,
   He has vanquished sin and Satan:
   He by death has spoiled his foes.
       While he lifts his hands in blessing,
       He is parted from his friends;
       While their eager eyes behold him,
       He upon the clouds ascends.

3. Thou hast raised our human nature
   On the clouds to God's right hand:
   There we sit in heavenly places,
   There with thee in glory stand.
       Jesus reigns, adored by angels;
       Man with God is on the throne;
       Mighty Lord, in thine ascension,
       We by faith behold our own.

80. Hail, thou once despised Jesus

John Blackwell and
Martin Madan

1. Hail, thou once despised Jesus!
   Hail, thou Galilean King!
   Thou didst suffer to release us;
   Thou didst free salvation bring.
      Hail, thou universal Saviour,
      Bearer of our sin and shame.
      By thy merit we find favour:
      Life is given through thy name.

2. Paschal Lamb, by God appointed,
   All our sins on thee were laid:
   By almighty love anointed,
   Thou hast full atonement made.
      All thy people are forgiven
      Through the virtue of thy blood:
      Opened is the gate of heaven,
      Peace is made 'twixt man and God.

3. Jesus, hail! enthroned in glory,
   There for ever to abide;
   All the heavenly hosts adore thee,
   Seated at thy Father's side.
      There for sinners thou art pleading:
      There thou dost our place prepare;
      Ever for us interceding,
      Till in glory we appear.

4. Worship, honour, power, and blessing
   Thou art worthy to receive:
   Highest praises, without ceasing,
   Meet it is for us to give.
      Help, ye bright angelic spirits,
      Bring your sweetest, noblest lays;
      Help to sing our Saviour's merits,
      Help to chant Emmanuel's praise!

81. He signed my deed

Anon.

He signed my deed with his atoning blood,
He ever lives to make his promise good.
Though all the hosts of hell march in to make a second claim,
They'll all march out at the mention of his name.

Three times.

82. Jesus is Lord

David J. Mansell

1. "Jesus is Lord!" Creation's voice proclaims it,
   For by his power each tree and flower was planned and
   made.

   "Jesus is Lord!" The universe declares it.
   Sun, moon and stars in heaven cry "Jesus is Lord!"

   Refrain
   Jesus is Lord! Jesus is Lord!
   Praise him with "Hallelujahs" for Jesus is Lord!

2. Jesus is Lord! Yet from his throne eternal
   In flesh he came to die in pain on Calvary's tree.
   Jesus is Lord! From him all life proceeding,
   Yet gave his life a ransom thus setting us free.

3. Jesus is Lord! O'er sin the mighty conqueror,
   From death he rose and all his foes shall own his name.
   Jesus is Lord! God sends his Holy Spirit
   To show by works of power that Jesus is Lord.

83. The joy of the Lord

Allienne G. Vale

1. The joy of the Lord is my strength. *Four times*

Refrain
A-ha-ha-ha... *Ls. 1-3*
The joy of the Lord is my strength.

2. If you want joy you must sing for it,
    If you want joy you must shout for it;
    If you want joy you must jump for it.
    The joy of the Lord is my strength.

3. The word of faith is nigh thee, even in thy mouth.

    Three times

    The joy of the Lord is my strength.

84. I heard the Lord

Jacob Krieger

1. I heard the Lord
    Call my name,
    Listen close,
    You'll hear the same.
    I heard the Lord
    Call my name,
    Listen close,
    You'll hear the same.
    I heard the Lord
    Call my name,
    Listen close,
    You'll hear the same.
    Take his hand
    We are glory bound.

2. His word is love,
    Love's his word,
That's the message
    That I heard.
Take his hand,
We are glory bound.

Place your hand in his and
    You will know
He will show you
    Where to go.

3. I felt his love
    From above
Settle on me
    Like a dove.
Take his hand,
We are glory bound.

4. And to the Father
    All your days
With the Son
    And Spirit praise.
Take his hand,
We are glory bound.

Place your hand in his and
You will know,
He will show you
    Where to go.

5. *Repeat verse 1.*

85.

And can it be?

Charles Wesley

1. And can it be that I should gain
   An interest in the Saviour's blood?
   Died he for me, who caused his pain?
   For me, who him to death pursued?
   Amazing love! how can it be
   That thou, my God, shouldst die for me?

2. 'Tis mystery all! th'immortal dies!
   Who can explore his strange design?
   In vain the firstborn seraph tries
   To sound the depths of love divine!
   'Tis mercy all! let earth adore,
   Let angel minds inquire no more.

3. He left his father's throne above,
   So free, so infinite his grace;
   Emptied himself of all but love,
   And bled for Adam's helpless race;
   'Tis mercy all, immense and free;
   For, O my God, it found out me.

4. Long my imprisoned spirit lay
   Fast bound in sin and nature's night;
   Thine eye diffused a quickening ray,
   I woke, the dungeon flamed with light;
   My chains fell off, my heart was free;
   I rose, went forth, and followed thee.

5. No condemnation now I dread;
   Jesus and all in him, is mine!
   Alive in him, my living head,
   And clothed in righteousness divine,
   Bold I approach the eternal throne,
   And claim the crown, through Christ my own.

86. Alleluia! Sons of God, arise!

Mimi Armstrong Farra

Refrain
Alleluia! Alleluia!
Alleluia, sons of God, arise.
Alleluia! Alleluia! Sons of God,
Arise and follow the Lord.

1. Come and be clothed in his righteousness;
   Come join the band who are called by his name.

2. Look at the world which is bound by sin;
   Walk into the midst of it proclaiming my life.

87. Come and go with me

Anon.

1. Come and go with me to my Father's house,
   to my Father's house, to my Father's house.
   Come and go with me to my Father's house
   where there's joy, joy, joy.

2. It's not very far to my Father's house...

3. There is room for all in my Father's house...

4. Everything is free in my Father's house...

5. Jesus is the way to my Father's house...

6. Jesus is the light in my Father's house...

88. Ho! everyone that thirsteth

Isaiah 55: 1-2

Refrain
Ho! everyone that thirsteth, come ye to the waters,
and he that hath no money, come ye, buy and eat.

1. Come, buy without money;
     come, buy without price.
   Come, buy milk and honey
     from Jesus Christ.

2. Wherefore do you spend money
     for that which is not bread;
   and your labour for that which satis-
     -fieth not?

2. Hearken unto me and
     eat that which is good;
   let your soul delight itself in
     fatness, fatness, fatness.

89. The sea walker

Anon.

Take my hand and follow me
To see the sea walker, the blind man healer,
The leper-cleansing man of Galilee.
He's the soul-saver, the one who set me free,
Take my hand and follow me.

90. O Lord, all the world belongs to you

Patrick Appleford

1. O Lord, all the world belongs to you,
   And you are always making all things new.
   What is wrong you forgive, and the new life you give
   Is what's turning the world upside down.

2. The world's only loving to its friends,
   But your way of loving never ends;
   Loving enemies too, and this loving with you
   Is what's turning the world upside down.

3. This world lives divided and apart;
   You draw men together and we start
   In your body to see that in fellowship we
   Can be turning the world upside down.

4. The world wants the wealth to live in state,
   But you show a new way to be great:
   Like a servant you came, and if we do the same,
   We'll be turning the world upside down.

5. O Lord, all the world belongs to you,
   And you are always making all things new,
   Send your Spirit on all in your Church whom you call
   To be turning the world upside down.

91.   Peace is flowing

Anon.

Peace is flowing like a river,
Flowing out through you and me,
Spreading out into the desert,
Setting all the captives free.

92.   God is working his purpose out

Arthur Ainger

1. God is working his purpose out
   As year succeeds to year:
   God is working his purpose out,
   And the time is drawing near;
   Nearer and nearer draws the time;
   The time that shall surely be,
   When the earth shall be filled with the glory of God
   As the waters cover the sea.

2. From utmost east to utmost west.
   Where'er man's foot hath trod,
   By the mouth of many messengers
   Goes forth the voice of God;
   Give ear to me, ye continents,
   Ye isles, give ear to me,
   That the earth may be filled with the glory of God
   As the waters cover the sea.

3. March we forth in the strength of God,
   With the banner of Christ unfurled,
   That the light of the glorious gospel of truth
   May shine throughout the world;
   Fight we the fight with sorrow and sin
   To set their captives free,
   That the earth may be filled with the glory of God
   As the waters cover the sea.

4. All we can do is nothing worth
   Unless God blesses the deed;
   Vainly we hope for the harvest tide
   Till God gives life to the seed;
   Yet nearer and nearer draws the time,
   The time that shall surely be,
   When the earth shall be filled with the glory of God
   As the waters cover the sea.

93. Go tell everyone

Alan Dale

1. God's Spirit is in my heart,
      He has called me and set me apart.
   This is what I have to do,
      What I have to do:

Refrain
He sent me to give the good news to the poor,
   Tell prisoners that they are prisoners no more;
Tell blind people that they can see,
   And set the down-trodden free.
And go tell everyone the news that the kingdom of God has
                                                    come,
   And go tell everyone the news that God's kingdom has
                                                    come.

2. Just as the Father sent me
      So I'm sending you out to be
   My witness throughout the world,
      The whole of the world.

3. Don't carry a load in your pack,
      You don't need two shirts on your back,
   A workman can earn his own keep,
      Can earn his own keep.

72   SOUND OF LIVING WATERS

4. Don't worry what you have to say,
    Don't worry because on that day
   God's Spirit will speak in your heart,
    Will speak in your heart.

94. O Zion, haste

Mary Ann Thompson

1. O Zion, haste, thy mission high fulfilling,
    To tell to all the world that God is light,
   That he who made all nations is not willing
    One soul should perish, lost in shades of night:

Refrain
Publish glad tidings: tidings of peace,
 Tidings of Jesus, redemption and release.

2. Proclaim to every people, tongue, and nation
    That God, in whom they live and move, is love;
   Tell how he stooped to save his lost creation,
    And died on earth that man might live above.

3. Give of thy sons to bear the message glorious;
    Give of thy wealth to speed them on their way;
   Pour out thy soul for them in prayer victorious
    Till God shall bring his kingdom's joyful day.

4. He comes again! O Zion, ere thou meet him,
    Make known to every heart his saving grace;
   Let none whom he hath ransomed fail to greet him,
    Through thy neglect, unfit to see his face.

95. **God has spoken**
"Song of good news"

W. F. Jabusch

Refrain
God has spoken to his people, hallelujah!
And his words are words of wisdom, hallelujah!

1. Open your ears, O Christian people,
    Open your ears and hear good news.
   Open your hearts, O royal priesthood,
    God has come to you.

2. He who has ears to hear his message,
    He who has ears, then let him hear.
   He who would learn the way of wisdom,
    Let him hear God's word.

3. Israel comes to greet the Saviour;
    Judah is glad to see his day.
   From east and west the peoples travel,
    He will show the way.

96. **Go forth and tell**

J. E. Seddon

1. Go forth and tell! O Church of God awake!
    God's saving news to all the nations take.
   Proclaim Christ Jesus, Saviour, Lord, and King,
    That all the world his worthy praise may sing.

2. Go forth and tell! God's love embraces all:
    He will in grace respond to all who call.
   How shall they call if they have never heard
    The gracious invitation of his word?

3. Go forth and tell! Men still in darkness lie:
   In wealth or want, in sin they live and die.
   Give us, O Lord, concern of heart and mind,
   A love like thine which cares for all mankind.

4. Go forth and tell! The doors are open wide:
   Share God's good gifts with men so long denied.
   Live out your life as Christ, your Lord, shall choose,
   Your ransomed powers for his sole glory use.

5. Go forth and tell! O Church of God, arise:
   Go in the strength which Christ your Lord supplies
   Go, till all nations his great name adore
   And serve him Lord and King for evermore.

97.　　　　　Joy in the Lord

(Psalm 100)

Jane Trigg

Refrain
Joy in the Lord,
O be joyful in the Lord,
All ye lands.

1. Serve the Lord with gladness.
   Come before him with a song.

2. Be sure the Lord is God.
   He has made us, we are his.

3. O go into his courts
   With thanksgiving and praise.

4. Be thankful unto him,
   And speak good of his name.

5. The Lord is gracious,
   Merciful for evermore.

98. Behold, how good and how pleasant it is

(Psalm 133)

Refrain
> Behold how good and how pleasant it is
> for brethren to dwell together in unity.

1. It is like the precious ointment upon the head
   that ran down upon the beard, even Aaron's beard,
   that ran down to the skirts of his garments;

2. As the dew of Hermon and as the dew
   that descended upon the mountain of Zion,
   for there the Lord commanded blessing.

3. For there the Lord commanded,
   commanded the blessing,
   even life for evermore.

99. The Lord has done great things for us

(Psalm 126)

1. When the Lord restored the fortunes of Zion,
   we were like those who dream.
   Then our mouths were filled with laughter,
   and our tongues with shouts of joy!

Refrain
> The Lord has done great things for us
> and we are glad.

2. Then they said among the nations,
   'The Lord has done great things for us.'

3. Restore our fortunes, O Lord,
      as the water courses in the Negeb.
   May those who sow in tears,
      reap with shouts of joy!

4. He that goes forth weeping
      bearing the seed for sowing,
   shall come home with shouts of joy,
      bringing his sheaves with him.

100.   The Lord hath put a new song
(Psalm 40)

Mimi Armstrong Farra

Refrain
The Lord hath put a new song in my mouth,
   in my mouth, in my mouth.
The Lord hath put a new song in my mouth,
   even praise unto our God.

1. And many shall see it and fear and trust,
      fear and trust, fear and trust,
   And many shall see it and fear and trust,
      and shall trust in the Lord.

2. I delight to do thy will, oh God,
      thy will, oh God, thy will, oh God,
   I delight to do thy will, oh God.
      Thy law is within my heart.

3. I have not hid thy righteousness within my heart,
      within my heart, within my heart.
   I have not hid thy righteousness within my heart.
      I have declared thy salvation.

4. I've not concealed thy loving kindness and thy truth,
   and thy truth, and thy truth,
   I've not concealed thy loving kindness and thy truth,
   from the great congregation.

5. So let thy loving kindness and thy truth,
   and thy truth, and thy truth,
   so let thy loving kindness and thy truth
   continually preserve me.

6. Let all those that seek thee rejoice and be glad
   rejoice and be glad, rejoice and be glad.
   Let all those that seek thee rejoice and be glad
   rejoice and be glad in thee.

Refrain
The Lord hath put a new song in my mouth,
   in my mouth, in my mouth.
The Lord hath put a new song in my mouth
   even praise unto our God.

101.   **As a doe**

(Psalm 42)

Mike Fitzgerald

Refrain
As a doe longs for running streams,
so longs my soul for you, my God.

1. My soul is thirsting for the God of life;
   when shall I see him face to face?
   I have no food but tears day and night;
   and men say, "Where is your God?"

2. I remember and my soul melts within.
      I'm on my way to the house of God,
   among cries of joy and praise;
      place your trust in God.

3. Why so downcast, O my soul?
      Why do you sigh so deep within?
   Place your hope in the God of life.
      I shall praise him again.

4. When I find my soul downcast within,
      I think of you, O mount Zion.
   Deep calls to deep as your waters roar;
      over me all your waves pour.

102.   The Lord's my shepherd

(Psalm 23)

Jessie Seymour Irvine

1. The Lord's my shepherd, I'll not want;
      He makes me down to lie
   In pastures green; he leadeth me
      The quiet waters by.

2. My soul he doth restore again:
      And me to walk doth make
   Within the paths of righteousness,
      E'en for his own name's sake.

3. Yea, though I walk in death's dark vale,
      Yet will I fear none ill;
   For thou art with me; and thy rod
      And staff me comfort still.

4. My table thou hast furnished
   In presence of my foes;
   My head thou dost with oil anoint,
   And my cup overflows.

5. Goodness and mercy all my life
   Shall surely follow me:
   And in God's house for evermore
   My dwelling-place shall be.

103. Sing a new song to the Lord

(Psalm 98)

Timothy Dudley-Smith

1. Sing a new song to the Lord,
   He to whom wonders belong!
   Rejoice in his triumph and tell of his power,
   O sing to the Lord a new song!

2. Now to the ends of the earth
   See his salvation is shown!
   And still he remembers his mercy and truth.
   Unchanging in love to his own.

3. Sing a new song and rejoice,
   Publish his praises abroad!
   Let voices in chorus, with trumpet and horn,
   Resound for the joy of the Lord!

4. Join with the hills and the sea
   Thunders of praise to prolong!
   In judgement and justice he comes to the earth,
   O sing to the Lord a new song!

104. Bless thou the Lord
(Psalm 103)

Refrain
Bless thou the Lord, O my soul, *Three times*
and forget not all his benefits.

1. Who forgiveth all thine iniquities,
   who healeth all thy diseases.

2. Who redeemeth thy life from destruction,
   who crowneth thee with loving kindness.

3. The Lord is merciful and gracious,
   slow to anger and plenteous in mercy.

4. For as the heaven is high above the earth,
   so great his mercy toward them that fear him

5. Like as a father pitieth his children,
   so the Lord pitieth them that fear him.

105. I rejoiced when I heard them say
(Psalm 122)

Betty Pulkingham

Refrain
I rejoiced when I heard them say,
   "Let us go to God's house today!"
I rejoiced when I heard them say,
   "Let us go to God's house."

1. And now our feet are standing.
     standing within thy gates,
   O Jerusalem.

2. Jerusalem is built as a city,
   it is there that the tribes go up,
   The tribes of the Lord.

3. For the peace of Jerusalem pray,
   peace be to your homes,
   Peace to your homes alway.

4. For love of my brethren and friends,
   for love of the house of the Lord,
   I will say, "Peace, peace upon you."

After final refrain:
   Let us go to God's house.

106. The butterfly song

Brian Howard

1. If I were a butterfly,
   I'd thank you, Lord, for giving me wings.
   And if I were a robin in a tree,
   I'd thank you, Lord, that I could sing.
   And if I were a fish in the sea,
   I'd wiggle my tail and I'd giggle with glee,
   But I just thank you, Father, for making me "me".

Refrain
For you gave me a heart and you gave me a smile.
You gave me Jesus and you made me your child.
And I just thank you, Father, for making me "me"

2. If I were an elephant,
   I'd thank you, Lord, by raising my trunk,
   And if I were a kangaroo,
   You know I'd hop right up to you
   And if I were an octopus,
   I'd thank you, Lord, for my fine looks,
   But I just thank you, Father, for making me "me".

3. If I were a wiggly worm,
    I'd thank you, Lord, that I could squirm.
And if I were a billy goat
    I'd thank you Lord for my strong throat,
And if I were a fuzzy-wuzzy bear,
    I'd thank you, Lord, for my fuzzy-wuzzy hair,
But I just thank you, Father, for making me "me".

107. Jesus, Jesus is my Lord

John Franklin
Age 12

Refrain
Jesus, Jesus is my Lord;
Always obey what Jesus says.

1. That's the way to lay down your life,
    Always obey what Jesus says.
The ones who come for Jesus' life,
    always obey what Jesus says.

2. He rewards you, making you free, always...
    And then you have power over the enemy, always...

3. He has given his Spirit to you, always...
    So keep his words and he will keep you, always...

108. The Lord is my shepherd
(2-part round)

Anon.

The Lord is my shepherd,
　I'll follow him alway.
He leads me by still waters
　I'll follow him alway.
Alway, alway,
　I'll follow him alway.
Alway, alway,
　I'll follow him alway.

109. Oh, how I love Jesus
Refrain: F. Whitfield

Question: Hey, (name) do you love Jesus?
Answer:　Yes, I love Jesus.
Q:　　　Are you sure you love Jesus?
A:　　　Yes, I'm sure I love Jesus.
Q:　　　Tell me, why do you love Jesus?
A:　　　This is why I love Jesus,
All:　　Because he first loved me,
　　　　　Yes, I love him,
　　　　　This is why I love him;

Refrain
Oh, how I love Jesus,
Oh, how I love Jesus,
Oh, how I love Jesus,
　Because he first loved me.
All:　　Yes, I love him, this is why I love him...

110.

Praise the Lord

('Sing, sing, praise and sing')

Elizabeth Syre

Refrain
Sing, sing, praise and sing!
Honour God for everything.
Glory to the highest king.
Sing and praise and sing!

1. Clap your hands, lift your voice,
   Praise the Lord and rejoice!

2. Full of joy, full of rest,
   In our Lord we are blessed.

3. Are you weak? Never mind!
   Come and sing, "God is kind!"

4. Love and peace is so near.
   Praise the Lord! God can hear!

5. Cymbal, harp, violin,
   Angels, priests, all join in.

111.

The body song

Betty Pulkingham
Adapted from 1 Cor. 12:14-26

1. If the eye say to the hand, "I have no need of thee."
   Or the head to the feet, "I have no need of you."
   Well, oh how can we write or hold a thimble?
   How can we walk or run so nimble?
   How can the body be complete without feet?
   How can the body be complete?

2. If the foot shall say, "Because I'm not the hand,
    I don't feel like a handsome part."
  Well, oh what does it matter to be first or to be latter?
    God has made the body whole and formed each part,
  God has made the body whole and formed each part.

3. If the ear shall say, "Because I'm not the eye,
    I don't seem to see things very clearly."
  Well, oh where were the hearing, and oh where were the
                                                smelling

    If the whole body were one single eye,
  If the whole body were one eye.

4. One single "I", it cannot be a body.
    One single "you" a body? "Nay!"
  Oh, God hath set the members,
    They are many, many members,
  Yet one body as it pleased him are they.
    Yet one body as it pleased him are they.

112.   **We love the Lord**

(David's song)

David Pulkingham
age 4

We love the Lord,
  Our neighbours and ourselves.
We open our eyes,
  We see him everywhere.
We love the Lord,
  Who died on the cross.
We love the Lord
  To love each other too.
We open our eyes,
  We see Jesus Christ;
He looks down at us,
  We look up at him.
We trust in him
  Eternally.

113. Thank you, Lord

Diane Davis

1. Thank you, Lord, for this fine day, *Three times*
   Right where we are.

Refrain
Alleluia, praise the Lord.
Alleluia, praise the Lord.
Alleluia, praise the Lord,
Right where we are.

2. Thank you, Lord for loving us.

3. Thank you, Lord, for giving us peace.

4. Thank you, Lord, for setting us free.

5. Thank you, Lord, for games to play.

114. Jesus is a friend of mine

Paul Mazak
age 4

1. Jesus is a friend of mine,
      Praise him.
   Jesus is a friend of mine,
      Praise him.
   Praise him, praise him.
   Jesus is a friend of mine,
      Praise him.

2. Jesus died to set us free,
      Praise him.

3. He gave us the victory,
   Praise him.

4. Jesus is the King of kings,
   Praise him.

115.   The wedding banquet
Miriam Therese Winter

Refrain
I cannot come.
I cannot come to the banquet, don't trouble me now.
   I have married a wife, I have bought me a cow.
I have fields and commitments that cost a pretty sum.
   Pray, hold me excused, I cannot come.

1. A certain man held a feast on his fine estate in town,
   He laid a festive table and wore a wedding gown.
   He sent invitations to his neighbours far and wide,
   But when the meal was ready, each of them replied:

2. The master rose up in anger, called his servants by name,
   Said: "Go into the town, fetch the blind and the lame,
   Fetch the peasant and the pauper, for this I have willed,
   My banquet must be crowded, and my table must be
   filled."

3. When all the poor had assembled, there was still room to
   spare,
   So the master demanded: "Go search everywhere,
   To the highways and the byways, and force them to come
   in.
   My table must be filled before the banquet can begin."

4. Now God has written a lesson for the rest of mankind;
   If we're slow in responding, he may leave us behind.
   He's preparing a banquet for that great and glorious day.
   When the Lord and Master calls us, be certain not to say:

116.   **Wake up!**

Betty Pulkingham

Refrain
Wake up! Wake up! It's time to rise and sing the praise of
                                      Jesus,
    Allelu, alleluia.
It's time to rise, to sing, to shout, to bring him all your heart.
He'll do the bigger part, if you will only make a start.

1. In the days of Noah's family,
    The people didn't know what the score was eternally.
They ate, and drank, got married and then
    Their sons and their daughters did the same things
                                         again.

2. John came baptising in the wilderness;
    Preaching to those who their sins confessed.
But to those who came for strife and debate, he said,
    "Who told you to come here, you tribe of snakes!"

3. When Jesus came to John in the wilderness;
    John said, "I should be the one to come to you, I must
                                   confess!
For I baptise with water at the most,
    But you will baptise with the Holy Ghost!"

4. Jesus told a story of ten maidens fair;
    Five were wise and ready, five did not prepare.
Those girls had lamps, but oh, dear me!
    They had no oil to light them so that they could see.

5. What good is a lamp without any oil?
    What good is our life if we struggle and toil,
But cannot see God's kingdom here,
    And live the loving life of his Son so dear?

117. On Jordan's Bank

Charles Coffin
Tr. John Chandler

1. On Jordan's bank the Baptist's cry
      Announces that the Lord is nigh;
   Awake and hearken, for he brings
      Glad tidings of the King of kings.

2. Then cleansed be every breast from sin;
      Make straight the way for God within,
   And let each heart prepare a home
      Where such a mighty guest may come.

3. For thou art our salvation, Lord,
      Our refuge, and our great reward;
   Without thy grace we waste away
      Like flowers that wither and decay.

4. To heal the sick stretch out thine hand,
      And bid the fallen sinner stand;
   Shine forth, and let thy light restore
      Earth's own true loveliness once more.

5. All praise, eternal Son, to thee,
      Whose advent doth thy people free;
   Whom with the Father we adore
      And Holy Ghost for evermore.

118.   Calypso carol

Michael Perry

Intro: Geoff last 2 lines verse tune.

1. See him a'lying on a bed of straw;
   Draughty stable with an open door,
   Mary cradling the babe she bore;
   The prince of glory is his name.

Refrain
   Oh, now carry me to Bethlehem
   To see the Lord appear to men;
   Just as poor as was the stable then,
   The prince of glory when he came.

2. Star of silver sweep across the skies,
   Show where Jesus in the manger lies.
   Shepherds swiftly from your stupor rise
   To see the Saviour of the world.

3. Angels, sing again the song you sang,
   Bring God's glory to the heart of man;
   Sing that Bethl'hem's little baby can
   Be salvation to the soul.

4. Mine are riches from thy poverty,
   From thine innocence, eternity;
   Mine, forgiveness by thy death for me,
   Child of sorrow for my joy.

END — Repeat whole chorus

119.   Oh Mary, don't you weep

Mimi Armstrong Farra

Refrain
Oh, Mary don't you weep,
And Mary don't you cry.

1. Oh, little baby Jesus,
   Baby Jesus is gonna die, but...

2. Baby Jesus is gonna die,
   Gonna die that we might live for ever.

3. Oh, sing glory hallelujah,
   Glory, glory baby Jesus.

120.   See, amid the winter's snow
Edward Caswall

1. See amid the winter's snow,
   Born for us on earth below
   See the tender Lamb appears,
   Promised from eternal years.

Refrain
Hail, thou ever-blessed morn!
Hail redemption's happy dawn!
Sing through all Jerusalem:
Christ is born in Bethlehem.

2. Lo, within a manger lies
   He who built the starry skies,
   He who throned in height sublime,
   Sits amid the cherubim.

3. Say, ye holy shepherds, say,
   What your joyful news today;
   Wherefore have ye left your sheep
   On the lonely mountain steep?

4. 'As we watched at dead of night,
   Lo, we saw a wondrous light:
   Angels, singing peace on earth,
   Told us of the Saviour's birth.

5. Sacred infant, all divine,
   What a tender love was thine,
   Thus to come from highest bliss
   Down to such a world as this!

6. Teach, O teach us, holy child,
   By thy face so meek and mild,
   Teach us to resemble thee
   In thy sweet humility.

121. Go tell it on the mountain

North American spiritual

Refrain
Go tell it on the mountain,
   Over the hills and everywhere,
Go tell it on the mountain
   That Jesus Christ is born.

1. While shepherds kept their watching
   O'er silent flocks by night.
   Behold throughout the heavens
   There shone a holy light.

2. The shepherds feared and trembled
   When lo, above the earth
   Rang out the angel chorus
   That hailed the Saviour's birth.

3. Down in a lowly manger
   Our humble Christ was born,
   And God sent us salvation
   That blessed Christmas morn.

4. When I was a seeker,
   I sought both night and day;
   I asked the Lord to help me,
   And he showed me the way.

5. He made me a watchman
   Upon the city wall,
   And if I am a Christian,
   I am the least of all.

122.   **Let your light shine**

Shirley Lewis Brown

1. Let your light shine,
   Let your light shine,
   Let your light shine before men,
   That they may see,
   May see your good works,
   And glorify the Father,
   The Father,
   The Father who is in heaven.

2. Once there was darkness,
   Once there was darkness,
   Once there was darkness upon earth.
   Then God sent Jesus,
   Then God sent Jesus
   To light the way, the pathway,
   The pathway,
   The pathway back to God.

3. What did he tell us?
   What did he tell us?
   What did he tell us we should do?
   He said to love God,
      To love your neighbour,
   And serve him; let your light shine,
      Let your light shine,
   Let your light shine before men.

123. Wondrous love

Trad.

1. What wondrous love is this, O my soul, O my soul?
   What wondrous love is this, O my soul?
   What wondrous love is this that caused the Lord of bliss
   To bear the dreadful curse for my soul, for my soul,
   To bear the dreadful curse for my soul.

2. When I was sinking down, sinking down, sinking down,
   When I was sinking down, sinking down,
   When I was sinking down beneath God's righteous frown,
   Christ laid aside his crown for my soul, for my soul,
   Christ laid aside his crown for my soul.

3. To God and to the Lamb I will sing, I will sing
   To God and to the Lamb I will sing.
   To God and to the Lamb who is the great I AM,
   While thousands join the theme, I will sing, I will sing,
   While thousands join the theme, I will sing.

4. And when from death I'm free, I'll sing on, I'll sing on,
   And when from death I'm free, I'll sing on.
   And when from death I'm free, I'll sing and joyful be,
   And through eternity I'll sing on, I'll sing on,
   And through eternity I'll sing on.

124.   The King of glory

W. F. Jabusch

Refrain
The King of glory comes,
The nation rejoices.
Open the gates before him,
Lift up your voices.

1. Who is the King of glory; how shall we call him?
    He is Emmanuel, the promised of ages.

2. In all of Galilee, in city or village,
    He goes among his people curing their illness.

3. Sing then of David's son, our Saviour and brother;
    In all of Galilee was never another.

4. He gave his life for us, the pledge of salvation.
    He took upon himself the sins of the nation.

5. He conquered sin and death; he truly has risen,
    And he will share with us his heavenly vision.

125.   The foot washing song

Shirley Lewis Brown
Adapted from John 13

Refrain
Put on the apron of humility;
Serve your brother, wash his feet,
That he may walk in the way of the Lord,
Refreshed, refreshed.

1. At the last supper with his disciples Jesus rose from the
   table,
   Took a towel and a basin of water and stooped to wash
   their feet.

2. When Jesus knelt before him, Peter said, "Lord, do you
   wash my feet?"
   Jesus answered, "Now you don't understand, but later on
   you will."
   Still protesting, Peter said, "Lord, you must never wash
   my feet."
   Jesus answered, "If I don't wash you, you have no part
   of me."

3. Then said Peter, "Lord, not only my feet, but also my
   hands and my head."
   Jesus answered, "He who has washed need only wash
   his feet."

4. Then said Jesus, "Do you know what it is that I have done?
   You call me your master and Lord, and you speak the
   truth, for so I am.
   If I then, your master and Lord, have stooped to wash
   your feet,
   So ought you men also to wash the feet of one another."

5. No man is greater than his master, no messenger than he
   who sent him.
   If you men know these things then happy are you if you
   do them.

126. Were you there?

North American spiritual

1. Were you there when they crucified my Lord?
   Oh! Sometimes it causes me to tremble, tremble, tremble.
   Were you there when they crucified my Lord?

2. Were you there when they nailed him to the tree?
   Oh! Sometimes it causes me to tremble, tremble, tremble.
   Were you there when they nailed him to the tree?

3. Were you there when they laid him in the tomb?
   Oh! Sometimes it causes me to tremble, tremble, tremble.
   Were you there when they laid him in the tomb?

127.

This song is omitted for copyright reasons

128. Thine be the glory

Edmond Louis Budry
Tr. Richard Birch Hoyle

1. Thine be the glory, risen conquering Son,
   Endless is the victory thou o'er death hast won;
   Angels in bright raiment rolled the stone away,
   Kept the folded grave-clothes, where thy body lay.

Refrain
Thine be the glory, risen, conquering Son,
Endless is the victory thou o'er death hast won!

2. Lo, Jesus meets us, risen, from the tomb!
   Lovingly he greets us, scatters fear and gloom:
   Let the church with gladness hymns of triumph sing,
   For her Lord now liveth, death hath lost its sting.

3. No more we doubt thee, glorious prince of life;
   Life is nought without thee: aid us in our strife;
   Make us more than conquerors, through thy deathless
                                                   love;
   Bring us safe through Jordan to thy home above.

129 & 130. Christ the Lord is risen today
Charles Wesley

1. Christ the Lord is risen today: Hallelujah!
      Sons of men and angels say, "Hallelujah!"
   Raise your joys and triumphs high: Hallelujah!
      Sing ye heavens; thou earth reply, Hallelujah!

2. Love's redeeming work is done; Hallelujah!
      Fought the fight, the battle won, Hallelujah!
   Death in vain forbids him rise, Hallelujah!
      Christ hath opened paradise, Hallelujah!

3. Lives again our glorious King! Hallelujah!
      Where, O death, is now thy sting? Hallelujah!
   Once he died our souls to save, Hallelujah!
      Where thy victory, O grave? Hallelujah!

4. Soar we now where Christ has led, Hallelujah!
      Following our exalted Head; Hallelujah!
   Made like him, like him we rise; Hallelujah!
      Ours the cross, the grave, the skies; Hallelujah!

131. He will fill your hearts today

Refrain : Mrs. C. H. Morris
Verses : Betty Pulkingham

Refrain
He will fill your hearts today to overflowing,
As the Lord commanded you
'Bring your vessels not a few,'
He will fill your hearts today to overflowing
With his Holy Ghost and power.

1. When the day of Pentecost had come,
      The believers were gathered together,
   Were gathered together in one place,
      Of one mind as the Lord had commanded.

2. Suddenly a noise from the sky,
      Which sounded like a strong wind blowing,
   A strong wind blowing by,
      Filled the whole place, the noise kept on growing.

3. Then they looked up and saw,
      They saw what looked like tongues of fire,
   Tongues of fire spreading out,
      To each one, spreading out to all the people.

4. All of them were filled with the Holy Ghost,
      With the Holy Ghost and power.
   They began to speak in other languages,
      In other languages he gave them in that hour!

132. Come, Holy Ghost

Louis Lambillotte

1. Come, Holy Ghost creator blest,
    Vouchsafe within our souls to rest;
   Come with thy grace and heavenly aid,
    And fill the hearts which thou hast made,
   And fill the hearts which thou hast made.

2. To thee the comforter we cry;
    To thee the gift of God most high;
   The fount of life, the fire of love,
    The soul's anointing from above.

3. The sevenfold gifts of grace are thine,
    O finger of the hand divine.
   True promise of the Father thou,
    Who dost the tongue with speech endow.

4. Thy light to every sense impart,
    And shed thy love in every heart;
   Thine own unfailing might supply,
    To strengthen our infirmity.

5. Drive far away our ghostly foe,
    And thine abiding peace bestow;
   If thou be our preventing guide,
    No evil can our steps betide.

133. Planted wheat

Jeff Cothran

1. Planted wheat, within the wheatfields,
    waiting till the summer time is near.
   Growing wheat, above the ploughlands,
    showing that the Lord of lords is here.

Refrain
He comes to grow a new creation, calling out a holy nation,
    all who will believe, and all who will receive.

2.   Jesus rose, we cannot see him;
        he is seated at the Father's hand.
    Yet he walks within his harvest,
        men in love obeying his command.

3.   Jesus Christ is Lord of the harvest.
        Soon in glory he will come again,
    Bringing all his holy angels,
        gathering in the ripened sheaves of grain.

Fresh Sounds

FRESH SOUNDS

CONTENTS

1.   **Sanna**

San-na, san-na-ni-na,
  San-na, san-na, san-na.
San-na, san-na-ni-na,
  San-na, san-na, san-na.

San-na, san-na,
  San-na, san-na-ni-na,
San-na, san-na, san-na.

2.   **Hail to the Lord's anointed**

James Montgomery

1. Hail to the Lord's anointed,
      Great David's greater Son!
    Hail in the time appointed,
      His reign on earth begun!
    He comes to break oppression,
      To set the captive free;
    To take away transgression,
    And rule in equity.

2. He shall come down like showers
      Upon the fruitful earth,
    And love, joy, hope, like flowers,
      Spring in his path to birth:
    Before him on the mountains
      Shall peace, the herald go;
    And righteousness in fountains
      From hill to valley flow.

3. Kings shall bow down before him,
        And gold and incense bring;
    All nations shall adore him,
        His praise all people sing;
    For he shall have dominion
        O'er every sea and shore;
    His kingdom still increasing,
        A kingdom for evermore.

4. O'er every foe victorious,
        He on his throne shall rest;
    From age to age more glorious,
        All blessing and all-blest:
    The tide of time shall never
        His covenant remove;
    His name shall stand for ever,
        His changeless name of love.

3. Crown him with many crowns

George Job Elvey

1. Crown him with many crowns,
        The Lamb upon his throne;
    Hark! how the heav'nly anthem drowns
        All music but its own;
    Awake, my soul, and sing
        Of him who died for thee,
    And hail him as thy matchless King
        Through all eternity.

FRESH SOUNDS

2. Crown him the Son of God
    Before the worlds began,
  And ye, who tread where he hath trod,
    Crown him the Son of man;
  Who ev'ry grief hath known
    That wrings the human breast,
  And takes and bears them for his own,
    That all in him may rest.

3. Crown him the Lord of life,
    Who triumphed o'er the grave,
  And rose victorious in the strife
    For those he came to save;
  His glories now we sing
    Who died, and rose on high,
  Who died, eternal life to bring,
    And lives that death may die.

4. Crown him of lords the Lord,
    Who over all doth reign,
  Who once on earth, the incarnate Word,
    For ransomed sinners slain,
  Now lives in realms of light,
    Where saints with angels sing
  Their songs before him day and night,
    Their God, Redeemer, King.

5. Crown him the Lord of heav'n,
    Enthroned in worlds above;
  Crown him the King, to whom is giv'n
    The wondrous name of Love.
  Crown him with many crowns,
    As thrones before him fall,
  Crown him, ye kings, with many crowns,
    For he is King of all.

4.　　　**The God of Abraham praise**

Jewish Doxology
Para. Thomas Oliver

1. The God of Abraham praise,
   Who reigns enthroned above;
   Ancient of everlasting days,
   And God of love;
   To him uplift your voice,
   At whose supreme command
   From earth we rise, and seek the joys
   At his right hand.

2. He by himself hath sworn:
   I on his oath depend;
   I shall, on eagle wings up-borne,
   To heav'n ascend:
   I shall behold his face,
   I shall his power adore,
   And sing the wonders of his grace
   For ever more

3. There dwells the Lord, our King,
   The Lord, our righteousness,
   Triumphant o'er the world and sin,
   The Prince of peace;
   On Sion's sacred height
   His kingdom he maintains,
   And, glorious with his saints in light,
   For ever reigns.

4. The God who reigns on high
   The great archangels sing,
   And "Holy, Holy, Holy," cry,
   "Almighty King!
   Who was, and is, the same,
   And evermore shall be:
   Eternal Father, great I AM,
   We worship thee."

5. The whole triumphant host
   Give thanks to God on high:
   "Hail, Father, Son, and Holy Ghost!"
   They ever cry;
   Hail, Abraham's God and mine!
   I join the heav'nly lays;
   All might and majesty are thine,
   And endless praise.

5. Hallelujah! Gonna sing all about it
Roy Turner

Hallelujah! Gonna sing all about it.
   Hallelujah! Gonna shout all about it.
Hallelujah! Can't live without it,
   Praise God. (Praise God.)
Now I'm living in a new creation,
   Now I'm drinking at the well of salvation.
Now there is no condemnation,
   Praise God. (Praise God.)

6. Hallelujah, my father

Tim Cullen

Hallelujah, my father,
   For giving us your Son,
Sending him into the world
   To be given up for men,
Knowing we would bruise him
   And smite him from the earth.
Hallelujah, my father,
   In his death is my birth.
Hallelujah, my father,
   In his life is my life.

7. Praise my God with the tambourine

Diane Davis
Adapted from Judith 16:1, 13-19
Jerusalem Bible

Refrain
Praise my God with the tambourine;
Sing to the Lord with the cymbals.

1. I will sing a new song to my God.
   "You are great you are glorious,
   Wonderfully strong."

2. "May your whole creation serve you.
   When you speak, things come into being;
   No one can resist your voice."

3. "Should the mountains topple to mingle with the
   waves,
   Should rocks melt like wax before your face,
   To those who fear you, you would still be merciful."

8. The dancing heart

Roy Turner

1. David danced before the Lord, he danced with all his
            might;
   His heart was filled with holy joy, his spirit was so light.
   Michal through the window looked, to criticise did start,
   She didn't know that David had got a dancing heart.

Refrain
Oh, the Holy Ghost will set your feet-a-dancing!
The Holy Ghost will fill you through and through.
The Holy Ghost will set your feet a-dancing,
And set your heart a-dancing too!

2. David danced before the Lord to magnify his name;
   In God's almighty presence he felt no sense of shame;
   The oil of gladness flowed that day, it quickened every
            part;
   He hadn't only dancing feet, he had a dancing heart.

3. Out of Egypt long ago the Israelites were led;
   By a mighty miracle they all were kept and fed;
   Through the Red Sea they were brought, the waters stood
            apart,
   And God gave sister Miriam a dance down in her heart.

4. There was a celebration — upon the Red Sea shore;
   Timbrels rang, desert sands became a dancing floor;
   The people sang and praised God there, he made the gloom
            depart,
   And put a dance of love and joy a-deep down in their
            hearts.

5. The prodigal was far away — wandering out in sin,
   But he came back to Father's house and Father took him
                                                        in;
   He put a robe upon his son — the merriment did start,
   The prodigal got dancing shoes to match his dancing heart.

6. The father's house with music rang to welcome home
                                                the son;
   Wine was flowing full and free, all misery was gone;
   The elder brother looking on complained it wasn't fair;
   He hadn't got a dancing heart like all the others there.

7. Now many saints are cold and bound by unbelief today,
   They want the blessings of the Lord but worry what men
                                                        say;
   Oh, let the Lord have full control, from dead traditions
                                                        part,
   And he will set you free within, you'll have a dancing heart.

9.   Now let us sing

Traditional

Now let us sing,
    Sing 'til the power of the Lord comes down.
Now let us sing,
    Sing 'til the power of the Lord comes down.
Lift up your hands,
    Lift up your hands.
Don't be afraid.
    Don't be afraid.
Now let us sing 'til the power of the Lord comes down.

Now let us (praise, pray, love...)
                or
Lift up your (hearts, heads...)

10. Sing praise to the Lord for ever (Jacob's Song)

Jacob Krieger
Adapted by Mikel Kennedy

Refrain
Sing praise to the Lord for ever and ever,
Call unto him for hope and salvation.
Sing praise, alleluia, sing praise, allelu,
Sing praise, alleluia, sing praise, allelu.

1. Oh, sing praise to our Father in heav'n.
   Sing unto the Lord.

2. Oh, sing praise to the Son of God.
   Call unto his name.

3. Oh, sing praise to the Spirit of God.
   Sing to the Lord of life.

11. Sing, sing alleluia

Nancy Carr Newman

Refrain
Sing, sing alleluia,
   Sing glory Jesus Christ,
Sing, sing alleluia,
   Behold the Lamb of God.

1. He rules the heavens, master of the earth.
   All men now join together to praise the Lord.

2. Who is the King of glory? What is his name?
   Jesus of Nazareth is his name.

3. Come ye who seek the Lord, place your trust in him.
   Jesus will set you free to follow him.

12. Sing to the Lord

Don Fishel

Refrain
Sing to the Lord a new song,
   Sing to the Lord a new song,
Sing to the Lord, sing to the Lord a new song.

1. God made the world in seven days.
    Adam sinned and then all men fell away.
    Jesus came to redeem my soul.
       He died upon the cross
       And he made me whole!

2. God said to Moses, "Go and set my people free.
    I will be your guide, just always follow me."
    Moses led the people through the parted Red Sea,
       Then they sang, and they danced,
       And they had a jubilee!

3. Jesus said to Peter, "Come on, I'm calling you.
    I know the way is hard, but I'll always see you through."
    Peter said, "My Lord, I'm a sinful man."
       Then he threw down his net, and
       To the Lord he ran!

4. Come on my brother, won't you turn to Jesus now.
    He knows that you're a sinner
    But he loves you anyhow.
       Jesus paid the price for your salvation,
       Just call upon his name and you're a new creation!

13. We will sing to the Lord our God

Richard Gullen

Refrain
We will sing to the Lord our God,
    mighty and splendid is he!
We will sing to our Saviour and King,
    glorious in majesty.

1.   Here is the Lord, he is among us;
    Let us worship him together.
    Here is the Lord, he is among us;
    Let us praise him all together.

2.   Here is the Lord, let us walk with him;
    He will lead and guide us through his land.
    Here is the Lord, let us walk with him;
    We will walk in peace throughout his land.

14. This is the day of the Lord

Charles High

This is the day of the Lord
    This is the day of the Lord.
This is the day of the Lord.
    Allelu, allelu.

Adapt verses to suit occasion, such as:

This is the (feast, birthday, service, song)
    of the Lord...

We are the people of the Lord...

These are the praises of the Lord...

15. Turn me, O God

Jodi Page

Refrain
Turn me, O God, and I shall be turned.
Turn me, O God, and I shall be turned.

1. Though I wander through desolation,
    I will find you there.
    Though the waters o'erwhelm my soul,
    Even so you are Lord.

2. Create in me a new heart.
    I would see your face.
    Take not your holy Spirit from me,
    I would see your face.

3. You have led us out of bondage,
    You have kept us well.
    Even in the face of our complaint,
    You have loved us still.

16. Jesus, I love you

Kathleen Thomerson

Refrain
Jesus, I love you.
    Jesus, I love you.
Jesus, I love you,
    Take my life.

1. Life is your gift, I give my heart.
    Kneel and adore You,
    And I know that

2. Now I have seen the love of God.
   He has poured out the Spirit of truth.

3. Love reaches out both near and far.
   And so we follow where you lead us.
   Jesus, I follow, Jesus, I follow,
   Jesus, I follow, all my life.

17. Jesus, Jesus
(2, 3, or 4-part round)

Anon.

Jesus, Jesus,
   Let me tell you what I know.
You have given us your spirit,
   We love you so.

18. The shepherd of my soul

Kathleen Thomerson

1. I sing to the shepherd of my soul all the day
   As he leads me through this world.
   To follow him, to truly follow in his way
   Is to live a life of love.

Refrain
All I am I offer Jesus,
   Singing praises unto him.
Oh, my soul, gives thanks to Jesus
   For he is your shepherd-king.

2. I sing to the shepherd of my soul all the night
   For the path is clear to him.
   And when I sleep, he makes a shelter of his light;
   When I wake he leads me on.

3. All my life, O shepherd of my soul, I will sing
   With a heart that's full of joy.
   To follow you is just to trust that you will bring
   All your sheep into the fold.

19. Come into his presence

Anon.

Come into his presence singing 'Alleluia,
  Alleluia, Alleluia.'

Other verses may be added:
Come into his presence singing "Jesus is Lord,"...
Come into his presence singing "Worthy the Lamb,"...
Come into his presence singing "Glory to God,"...

20. My song is love unknown

Samuel Crossman

1. My song is love unknown,
     My Saviour's love to me,
   Love to the loveless shown,
     That they might lovely be,
   O who am I, that for my sake
     My Lord should take frail flesh and die?

2. He came from his blest throne
     Salvation to bestow;
   But men made strange, and none
     The longed for Christ would know.
   But O, my friend, my friend indeed,
     Who at my need his life did spend.

3. Sometimes they strew his way
    And his sweet praises sing;
Resounding all the day
    Hosannas to their King.
Then crucify is all their breath,
    And for his death they thirst and cry.

4. They rise and needs will have
    My dear Lord made away;
A murderer they save,
    The Prince of life they slay,
Yet cheerful he to suffering goes,
    That he his foes from thence might free.

5. In life, no house, no home
    My Lord on earth might have;
In death, no friendly tomb,
    But what a stranger gave.
What may I say? Heaven was his home;
    But mine the tomb wherein he lay.

6. Here might I stay and sing,
    No story so divine;
Never was love, dear King,
    Never was grief like thine.
This is my friend, in whose sweet praise
    I all my days could gladly spend.

21. I love the name of Jesus

Kathleen Thomerson

1. I love the name of Jesus, King of my heart,
    He is everything to me.
I bless the name of Jesus, reign in my life,
    show the Father's love so free.
Spirit of love, spirit of power,
    shine through eternity.
I love the name of Jesus, light of the world,
    let me walk each day with thee.

2. I love the name of Jesus, risen above,
   and he loves and prays for me.
   I bless the name of Jesus, ruling on high
   with a glorious majesty.
   Spirit of love, spirit of power,
   shine through eternity.
   I praise the name of Jesus, Lord of my life,
   for he died to set me free.

3. I love the name of Jesus, splendour of God,
   and his face I long to see.
   I bless the name of Jesus, shepherd of men;
   by his side I now can be.
   Spirit of love, spirit of power,
   shine through eternity.
   I praise the name of Jesus, for he is love,
   and that love he gives to me.

22.   Blessed be the name

Anon.

1. Blessed be the name, blessed be the name,
   Blessed be the name of the Lord.

2. Jesus is the name, Jesus is the name,
   Jesus is the name of the Lord.

3. Worthy to be praised, worthy to be praised,
   Worthy to be praised is the Lord.

23. Glory

Mimi Armstrong Farra

1. Sing to the Lord,
       Sing to the Lord of Lords.
    Glory, glory,
       Glory, glory,
    Glory to the Lord.

2. Sing, oh sing to the Son of God,
       Sing, for he is worthy of
    Glory, glory,
       Glory, glory,
    Glory to the Son.

3. Sing, oh sing to the Lamb of God,
       Sing, for he is worthy of
    Glory, glory,
       Glory, glory,
    Glory to the Lamb.

4. Sing, oh sing to the Word of God,
       The Word made flesh in Jesus Christ.
    Glory, glory,
       Glory, glory,
    Glory Jesus Christ.

24. Sweet Jesus

Anon.

1. Sweet Jesus, sweet Jesus,
       Lily of the valley,
       Bright as the morning star.
    Sweet Jesus, sweet Jesus,
       He's the God of every nation,
       Bless his name.

2. How I love him, how I love him,
      Lily of the valley,
      Bright as the morning star.
    How I love him, how I love him,
      He's the God of every nation,
      Bless his name.

3. Jesus loves you...

4. Sweet Jesus...

25.   **Sweet Jesus**

                                          Paul Goodwin

Sweet Jesus, sweet Jesus,
  What a wonder you are,
  You are brighter than the morning star;
You are fairer, much fairer
  Than the lily that grows by the wayside,
  Precious, more precious than gold.

You are the rose of Sharon,
The fairest of the fair,
You are all my heart could e'er desire.

Sweet Jesus, sweet Jesus,
  What a wonder you are,
  You are precious, more precious than gold.

26. God gives peace like a river

Anon.

God gives peace like a river, peace like a river,
   God gives peace like a river in my soul.
God gives peace like a river, peace like a river,
   God gives peace like a river in my soul.

God gives love...
God gives joy...
God gives faith...
God gives hope...
God gives praise...

27. O worship the Lord in the beauty of holiness

John S. B. Monsell

1. O worship the Lord in the beauty of holiness,
    Bow down before him, his glory proclaim!
  With gold of obedience, and incense of lowliness,
    Kneel and adore him, the Lord is his name.

2. Low at his feet lay thy burden of carefulness,
    High on his heart he will bear it for thee,
  Comfort thy sorrows and answer thy prayerfulness,
    Guiding thy steps as may best for thee be.

3. Fear not to enter his courts in the slenderness
    Of the poor wealth thou would'st reckon as thine!
  Truth in its beauty, and love in its tenderness,
    These are the offerings to lay on his shrine.

4. These, though we bring them in trembling and
                    fearfulness,
    He will accept for the name that is dear;
    Mornings of joy give for evenings of tearfulness,
    Trust for our trembling, and hope for our fear.

5. O worship the Lord in the beauty of holiness,
   Bow down before him, his glory proclaim!
   With gold of obedience, and incense of lowliness,
   Kneel and adore him, the Lord is his name.

28.   My Jesus, I love thee

W. R. Featherston

1. My Jesus, I love thee, I know thou art mine,
   For thee all the follies of sin I resign.
   My gracious Redeemer, my Saviour art thou:
   If ever I loved thee, my Jesus, 'tis now.

2. I love thee because thou hast first loved me
   And purchased my pardon on Calvary's tree.
   I love thee for wearing the thorns on thy brow:
   If ever I loved thee, my Jesus, 'tis now.

3. I'll love thee in life, I will love thee in death,
   And praise thee as long as thou lendest me breath;
   And say when the death dew lies cold on my brow:
   If ever I loved thee, my Jesus, 'tis now.

4. In mansions of glory and endless delight,
   I'll ever adore thee in heaven so bright;
   I'll sing with the glittering crown on my brow:
   If ever I loved thee, my Jesus, 'tis now.

29.   Turn your eyes upon Jesus

H. H. Lemmel

Turn your eyes upon Jesus,
   Look full in his wonderful face;
And the things of earth will grow strangely dim
   In the light of his glory and grace.

30. Jesus, the very thought of thee

Tr. Edward Caswall

1. Jesus, the very thought of thee
    With sweetness fills the breast:
    But sweeter far thy face to see,
    And in thy presence rest.

2. No voice can sing, no heart can frame,
    Nor can the memory find,
    A sweeter sound than Jesus' name,
    The Saviour of mankind.

3. O hope of every contrite heart,
    O joy of all the meek,
    To those who fall, how kind thou art!
    How good to those who seek!

4. But what to those who find? Ah, this
    No tongue nor pen can show;
    The love of Jesus, what it is,
    None but his loved ones know.

5. Jesus, our only joy be thou,
    As thou our prize will be;
    In thee be all our glory now.
    And through eternity.

31. My God, how wonderful thou art

Frederick William Faber

1. My God, how wonderful thou art,
    Thy majesty how bright!
    How beautiful thy mercy seat,
    In depths of burning light!

2. How dread are thine eternal years,
    O everlasting Lord,
  By prostrate spirits day and night
    Incessantly adored!

3. O how I fear thee, living God,
    With deepest tenderest fears,
  And worship thee with trembling hope,
    And penitential tears.

4. Yet I may love thee, too, O Lord,
    Almighty as thou art,
  For thou hast stooped to ask of me
    The love of my poor heart.

5. How wonderful, how beautful,
    The sight of thee must be,
  Thine endless wisdom, boundless power,
    And aweful purity.

32.

This hymn is omitted for copyright reasons.

33. # I will arise
Mimi Armstrong Farra

Refrain
I will arise so early in the morning,
Rise to sing my Saviour's praises;
Rise with joy in my heart to greet the Lord
Who gives me life, everlasting life.

1. Now no more can sorrow
    And death cause me to fear; for

2. I will sing to the God of creation;
    I will sing to the Lord of love.

128

Allelu

Mimi Armstrong Farra

1. Come and bless, come and praise,
     Come and praise the living God.
   Allelu, allelu, alleluia, Jesus Christ.

Refrain
Allelu, allelu, alleluia, Jesus Christ.
Allelu, allelu, alleluia, Jesus Christ.

2. Come and seek, come and find,
     Come and find the living God,
   Allelu, allelu, alleluia, Jesus Christ.

3. Come and hear, come and know,
     Come and know the living God.
   Allelu, allelu, alleluia, Jesus Christ.

4. Come and bless, come and praise,
     Come and praise the Word of God;
   Word of God, Word made flesh,
     Alleluia, Jesus Christ.

Seasonal verses:
5. Come behold, come and see,
     Come and see the newborn babe.
   Allelu, allelu, alleluia, Jesus Christ.

6. Angel choirs sing above,
     "Glory to the Son of God!"
   Shepherd folk sing below,
     "Allelu, Emmanuel!"

35. I trust in thee, O Lord
(Psalm 31)

M. McAllister

I trust in thee, O Lord.
  I say, "Thou art my God."
My times are in thy hand,
  My times are in thy hand.
Blessed be the Lord,
  For he has wondrously shown
His steadfast love to me,
  His steadfast love to me.

36. O magnify the Lord

Ruth Wieting
Based on Psalm 34

Refrain
O magnify the Lord with me,
Let us praise his name together.

1. I will bless the Lord at all times.
   His praise will always be in my mouth.

2. I cried unto the Lord,
    And he has freed me from all my fears.

3. O trust the Lord, you Saints,
   For those who trust him lack no good thing.

4. O come, you Sons of God
   To be the body of Jesus Christ.

37.   **There is a river**

Psalm 46:4-5

There is a river whose streams make glad
   The city of God, the city of God;
The holy habitation of the most high,
   The city of God, the city of God.
God is in the midst of her,
   She shall not be moved;
   The Lord of hosts is with her.

38.   **O give thanks unto the Lord**
(Psalm 136)

Refrain
O give thanks unto the Lord, for he is good,
   for his mercy endureth for ever.

1. O give thanks unto the God of Gods,
   for his mercy endureth for ever.
O give thanks unto the Lord of Lords,
   for his mercy endureth for ever.
To him who alone doeth great wonders,
   for his mercy endureth for ever.   *Refrain*

2. To him that by wisdom made the heav'ns,
   for his mercy . . .
To him that stretched the earth above the water,
   for his mercy . . .
To him that made great lights,
   for his mercy . . .   *Refrain*

3. To him that smote Egypt in their first-born,
       for his mercy . . .
   And brought out Israel from among them,
       for his mercy . . .
   With a strong hand and with a stretched out arm,
       for his mercy . . . *Refrain*

4. To him which divided the Red Sea,
       for his mercy . . .
   And made Israel to pass through the midst of it,
       for his mercy . . .
   But overthrew Pharoah and all his host,
       for his mercy . . . *Refrain*

5. To him which led his people through the wilderness,
       for his mercy . . .
   To him which smote great kings,
       for his mercy . . .
   And gave them land for an heritage,
       for his mercy . . . *Refrain*

6. Who remembered us in our low estate,
       for his mercy . . .
   And hath redeemed us from our enemies,
       for his mercy . . .
   O give thanks unto the God of heaven,
       for his mercy . . . *Refrain*

Christmas antiphon
7. Alleluia, Alleluia,
       for his mercy . . .
   Unto us is born a Son, Alleluia,
       for his mercy . . .
   And he shall rule with equity,
       for his mercy . . . *Refrain*

39.   **The song of Simeon**

(Nunc Dimittis)

Luke 2:29–32

Refrain
Lord, you have fulfilled your word;
Now let your servant depart in peace.

1. With my own eyes I have seen the salvation,
   Which you have prepared in the sight of every people:

2. A light to reveal you to the nations,
   And the glory of your people Israel.

40.   **My soul doth magnify the Lord**

Based on Luke 1:46, 47, 49

My soul doth magnify the Lord,
And my spirit hath rejoiced in God my Saviour
For he that is mighty hath done great things,
And holy is his name.

My soul doth magnify the Lord,
My soul doth magnify the Lord,
And my spirit hath rejoiced in God my Saviour
For he that is mighty hath done great things,
And holy is his name.

41.   Jesus, Lamb of God
(Agnus Dei)

Traditional

Jesus, Lamb of God,
   Have mercy on us.
Jesus, bearer of our sins,
   Have mercy on us.
Jesus, redeemer of the world,
    Give us your peace.
    Give us your peace.

42.   Calypso Doxology

Thomas Ken
Verse 2: Deanna Wheeler

1. Praise God from whom all blessings flow,
   praise him all ye creatures here below.
Praise him above, ye heavenly host,
   praise him Father, Son and Holy Ghost.

2. Hallelujah! Got the victory
   over Satan and over sin.
Jesus Christ is alive today, and he
   leads and guides me all the way.

3. Amen, amen, amen, amen, amen,
   amen, amen, amen, amen.
Amen, amen, amen, amen, amen,
   Amen, amen, amen, amen.

43. Tallis' Canon

Thomas Ken

Praise God from whom all blessings flow.
Praise him, all creatures here below.
Praise him above, ye heavenly host.
Praise Father, Son and Holy Ghost.

44. Doxology

Thomas Ken

Praise God from whom all blessings flow;
Praise him all creatures here below.
Praise him above ye heavenly hosts;
Praise Father, Son, and Holy Ghost.

45. The Lord's Prayer

Traditional

Our Father in heaven,
Hallowed be your name.
Your kingdom come, your will be done
On earth as in heaven.
Give us today our daily bread.
Forgive us our sins as we forgive
Those who sin against us.
Do not bring us to the time of trial
But deliver us from evil.
For the kingdom, the power and the glory
Are yours now and for ever. Amen.

46. Hallowed be thy name

Traditional

Our Father who art in heaven,
  Hallowed be thy name.
They kingdom come, thy will be done,
  Hallowed be thy name.
On the earth as it is in heaven,
  Hallowed be thy name.
Give us this day our daily bread,
  Hallowed be thy name.
And forgive us all our trespasses,
  Hallowed be thy name.
As we forgive those who trespass against us,
  Hallowed be thy name.
And lead us not to the devil to be tempted,
  Hallowed be thy name.
But deliver us from all that is evil.
  Hallowed be thy name.
For thine is the Kingdom and the power and the glory,
  Hallowed be thy name.
For ever and ever and ever,
  Hallowed be thy name.
Amen, amen, amen, amen,
  Hallowed be thy name.
Amen, amen, amen, amen,
  Hallowed be thy name.

47. The steadfast love of the Lord

Edith McNeill

Refrain
The steadfast love of the Lord never ceases,
   His mercies never come to an end.
They are new every morning, new every morning.
   Great is thy faithfulness, O Lord!
   Great is thy faithfulness.

1. The Lord is my portion, says my soul.
      Therefore I will hope in him.

2. The Lord is good to those who wait for him,
      To the soul that seeks him.
   It is good that we should wait quietly
      For the salvation of the Lord.

3. The Lord will not cast off for ever,
      But will have compassion.
   For he does not willingly afflict or grieve
      The sons of men.

4. So let us examine all our ways,
      And return to the Lord.
   Let us lift up our hearts and hands
      To God in heav'n.

48. Put on love

Jodi Page
Based on Col. 3:12-16

Refrain
Put on love, put on love,
And the peace of God that binds us all together
Will keep our hearts in perfect harmony,
   If we put on love.

1. We are God's chosen race, his saints,
       And he loves us.
    We should be clothed in peace,
       In kindness, and humility
    As we . . .

2. God has forgiven us,
       Now we should forgive our brother.
    We should show gentleness
       And bear with one another
    As we . . .

3. Always be thankful and
       Let the message of Jesus
    In all its richness
       Find a dwelling place in our hearts
    As we . . .

49.   I heard the voice of Jesus say

Horatius Bonar

1. I heard the voice of Jesus say,
    "Come unto me and rest;
    Lay down, thou weary one, lay down
    Thy head upon my breast."

    I came to Jesus as I was,
    Weary and worn and sad;
    I found in him a resting-place,
    And he has made me glad.

2. I heard the voice of Jesus say,
    "Behold I freely give
    The living water; thirsty one,
    Stoop down and drink, and live."

    I came to Jesus and I drank
    Of that life-giving stream;
    My thirst was quenched, my soul revived,
    And now I live in him.

3. I heard the voice of Jesus say,
    "I am this dark world's light;
    Look into me, thy morn shall rise,
    And all thy day be bright."

    I looked to Jesus, and I found
    In him, my star, my sun;
    And in that light of life I'll walk
    Till trav'ling days are done.

50.   There is power in the blood

Refrain: L. E. Jones
Verses: Gary Miles

1. My Jesus, he saves and heals me,
       My body, spirit, soul.
   My king and my shepherd leads me
       And makes my body whole.

Refrain
Oh, there is power, power, wonder-working power
    In the blood of the Lamb.
There is power, power, wonder-working power
    In the precious blood of the Lamb.

2. He fills me to over-flowing,
       He comes as the dove,
   My spirit and his united.
       Oh, wondrous, precious love.

3. Our Father, he made and loves us,
       He gave us his only Son.
   We'll see him one day in glory
       And join the Three in One.

51.   The man of Galilee

Linda Rich

1. They say that I'm a dreamer,
       Blind and cannot see
   That life consists of living
       Only to earn money.
   Well, you know who I am, Lord;
       You'll always care for me.
   I only want to be like the
       Man of Galilee.

Refrain
I want to be like,
I want to hear like,
I want to see like
The man of Galilee.

2. They say that I'm an idealist,
        Blind and cannot see
    That the principles I cling to
        Can't stand reality.
    Well, I know who you are, Lord;
        You'll always care for me.
    I only want to be like the
        Man of Galilee.

52.   **Wind, wind**

                                    Jane and Betsy Clowe

Refrain
Wind, wind, blow on me;
    Wind, wind, set me free:
Wind, wind, my Father sent
    The blessed Holy Spirit.

1. Jesus told us all about you,
        How we could not live without you,
    With his blood the power bought to
        Help us live the life he taught.

2. When we're weary you console us;
        When we're lonely you enfold us;
    When in danger you uphold us,
        Blessed Holy Spirit.

3. When unto the Church you came,
    It was not in your own but Jesus' name.
  Jesus Christ is still the same,
    He sends the Holy Spirit.

4. Set us free to love our brothers;
    Set us free to live for others
  That the world the Son might see
    And Jesus' name exalted be.

53. The fruit of the Spirit

Brian Casebow
Refrain: Gal. 5:22

Refrain
For the fruit of the Spirit is love, joy, peace,
  patience, kindness, goodness,
Faithfulness, gentleness, self-control;
  for such there is no law.

1. Have you seen my Lord on the cross so high?
   Do you know his name? Do you hear his cry?
   "Father, here's my love. Father, take my love,
     As the tree bears fruit for you."

2. Have you seen his face and the look he gave
   To the dying man he alone would save?
   "Sinner, here's my love. Sinner, take my love,
     As the tree bears fruit for you."

3. Can we answer him? Can the heart reply?
   How to follow him as we live and die!
   Jesus, here's our love. Jesus, take our love,
     As the tree bears fruit for you!

54. By their fruits ye shall know them

C + 3 (E♭)

Jon Wilkes
Based on Matt. 7:16

Refrain
Can men gather grapes from the thorns,
   Or figs from the thistled stem?
He that hath ears let him hear,
By their fruits ye shall know them.

1. My friend came to man to show him how to love;
     His blessing he gave to the meek.
    Men took his love and they called it a lie,
     His answer was only this cry:

Refrain

2. In darkness they led him to priests and kings,
     They called him the Lord of the Flies.
    Spat in his face and they crowned him with thorns:
     "Hail the King of the Jews."

Refrain

3. They nailed his hands and split his side,
     They cast the lots for his clothes.
    The only comfort they had to give
     Was vinegar and gall.

Modified Refrain
Can men gather grapes from the thorns,
   Or figs from the thistled stem?
Father, forgive, — they know not what they do; ← SOLO
By their fruits ye shall know them.

4. Brothers, oh judge the heart of mankind,
        The test is sure and true.
    Eat of the fruit and savour the taste.
        What does it say to you?

Refrain

& last line bis.

55.   **My God**
                        (A Psalm of Spring)

Nan Pagano

Refrain
My God makes the flowers to bloom.
My God sends the rain.
    My God sets the rainbow in the sky,
    Hears each baby when he cries,
    And each mother as she sighs,
    Sent his only Son to die.
Oh, praise him,
My God is the only true and living God
And he has made me his child.

1. One day in spring while walking with the Lord,
        Listening to his word, I heard him say,
    "This is my world and I have given it to you,
        Every colour, every hue,
    Every breeze and drop of dew is from my hand.
    Walk in the knowledge that the waters swirling round
    And the rocks resound
    The praises of my name."
    My heart cried,

2. When summer heat reveals the circumstance of life,
    The burden and the strife, call on my name.
   Then autumn comes and all your world is turning brown,
    The leaves are falling down
    And the winter's cold is all around. It's from my hand.
   Walk in the knowledge that the faith you have is seed
    Sufficient to the need,
    So claim my grace and live!
    My heart cried,

3. He spoke again and said, "You are a child of mine,
    A branch upon the vine. Bring forth my fruit."
   My heart cried out, "I see, it's all a gift from thee!
    Let the seasons have their way, Lord,
    Walk with me through night and day. It's from my hand.
   I'll walk in knowledge that the spring will come again
    And I will go rejoicing
    In the fragrance of its bloom."
    My heart cried,

56.   Israel is my vineyard

Marie Malone
Isa. 27:2-3

Israel is my vineyard and I, the Lord,
 Will tend the fruitful vines.
Every day I'll water them and day and night
 I'll watch to keep all enemies away. I'll...

Alleluia, alleluia, praise the Lord!
 Alleluia, praise his name!
Alleluia, alleluia, praise the Lord!
 Alleluia, praise his name.

57. Thou wilt keep him in perfect peace

Anon.

1. Thou wilt keep him in perfect peace,
   Thou wilt keep him in perfect peace,
   Thou wilt keep him in perfect peace
   Whose mind is stayed on thee.

2. Marvel not that I say unto you,
   Marvel not that I say unto you,
   Marvel not that I say unto you,
   Ye must be born again.

3. Though your sins as scarlet be,
   Though your sins as scarlet be,
   Though your sins as scarlet be,
   They shall be white as snow.

4. If the Son shall make you free,
   If the Son shall make you free,
   If the Son Shall make you free,
   Ye shall be free indeed.

5. They that wait upon the Lord,
   They wait upon the Lord,
   They that wait upon the Lord,
   They shall renew their strength.

6. Whom shall I send and who will go?
   Whom shall I send and who will go?
   Whom shall I send and who will go?
   Here I am, Lord, send me.

58. The Lord is a great and mighty king

Diane Davis

Refrain
The Lord is a great and mighty king,
   Just and gentle with every thing.
So with happiness we sing,
   And let his praises ring.

1. We are his voice, we his song;
       Let us praise him all day long. Alleluia!

2. We are his body here on earth;
       From above he gave us birth. Alleluia!

3. For our Lord we will stand,
       Sent by him to every land. Alleluia!

4. The Lord our God is one,
       Father, Spirit and the Son. Alleluia!

59. This is the feast

John Ylvisaker

Refrain
This is the feast of vict'ry for our God,
For the Lamb who was slain has begun his reign:
   Alleluia.

1. Worthy is Christ, the Lamb who was slain,
       Whose blood set us free to be people of God.
    Power, riches, wisdom and strength
       And honour, blessing and glory are his.

2. Sing with all the people of God
       And join in the hymn of all creation:
    "Blessing, honour, glory and might
       Be to God and the Lamb for ever. Amen."

60. Please break this bread, Lord

Jodi Page

Refrain
Please break this bread, Lord,
  Please break this bread,
Bread of your body risen in us.

Pour out your wine, Lord,
  Pour out your wine.
Let it flow through us to a thirsty world.

1. We've come to eat your bread,
      Make us one.
    We've come to drink your wine,
      Make us one.
    We've come in memory of your death
      To give you thanks.
    We've come to celebrate your life
      And give you praise.

2. Let us be broken, O Lord,
      To feed your sheep.
    Let us be poured out, O Lord,
      That men may see
    That you are Spirit and life
      That satisfy,
    That you are risen in us
      To set men free.

Last Refrain
Please break this bread, Lord,
  Please break this bread.
Pour out your wine, Lord,
  Pour out your wine.

61. Let us break bread together

Traditional

1. Let us break bread together, we are one.
   Let us break bread together, we are one.
   We are one as we stand with our face to the risen Son.
   Oh, Lord, have mercy on us.

2. Let us drink wine together, we are one.
   Let us drink wine together, we are one.
   We are one as we stand with our face to the risen Son.
   Oh, Lord have mercy on us.

3. Let us praise God together, we are one.
   Let us praise God together, we are one,
   We are one as we stand with our face to the risen Son.
   Oh, Lord, have mercy on us.

62. Who are my mother and my brothers?

Mark 3:35

Anyone who does the will of God,
   Anyone who does the will of God,
Anyone who does the will of God
   Is my brother, my sister and mother.

63.　Triumphant Zion

Philip Doddridge

1. Triumphant Zion, lift thy head
   From dust and darkness and the dead;
   Though humbled long, awake at length,
   And gird thee with thy Saviour's strength.

2. Put all thy beauteous garments on,
   And let thine excellence be known:
   Decked in the robes of righteousness,
   The world thy glories shall confess.

3. No more shall foes unclean invade,
   And fill thy hallowed walls with dread;
   No more shall hell's insulting host
   Their vict'ry and thy sorrows boast.

4. God from on high has heard thy prayer,
   His hand thy ruins shall repair:
   Nor will thy watchful monarch cease
   To guard thee in eternal peace.

64.　What could be better?

Brian Howard

1. What could be better than to come to dine
   On this bread and on this wine,
   The bread of life and the cup of suffering,
   The body and blood of Jesus, our King?
   I believe he's opened our eyes to really see
   There's nothing better than to come to dine in unity.

2. What could be better than to carry the cross
        That our Lord has given us?
    Just like his only begotten Son,
        He's chosen us to carry one.
    I believe he's opened our eyes to really see
    There's nothing better than to carry the cross in unity.

3. What could be better than to live in love
        With God's holy chosen ones,
    Living together in unity, and out of that life
        The world to feed?
    I believe he's opened our eyes to really see
    There's nothing better than to live together in unity.

4. What could be better than to follow the Lord?
        In this whole wide world, there's nothing I'm sure.
    So follow him we shall surely do.
        Listen, he's speaking to me and you.
    I believe he's opened our eyes to really see
    There's nothing better than to follow the Lord in unity.

65.   Guide me, O thou great Jehovah
William Williams

1. Guide me, O thou great Jehovah,
        Pilgrim through this barren land;
    I am weak, but thou art mighty.
        Hold me with thy powerful hand:
    Bread of heaven, Bread of heaven,
        Feed me now and evermore,
        Feed me now and evermore.

2. Open thou the crystal fountain
    Whence the healing stream doth flow;
Let the fiery cloudy pillar
    Lead me all my journey through:
Strong deliv'rer, strong deliv'rer,
    Be thou still my strength and shield,
    Be thou still my strength and shield.

3. When I tread the verge of Jordan
    Bid my anxious fears subside;
Death of death, and hell's destruction
    Land me safe on Canaan's side:
Songs of praises, songs of praises,
    I will ever give to thee,
    I will ever give to thee.

66.   God of grace and God of glory

Harry Emerson Fosdick

1. God of grace and God of glory,
    On thy people pour thy power;
Crown thine ancient Church's story;
    Bring her bud to glorious flower.
Grant us wisdom, grant us courage,
    For the facing of this hour.

2. Lo! the hosts of evil round us
    Scorn thy Christ, assail his ways!
From the fears that long have bound us
    Free our hearts to faith and praise:
Grant us wisdom, grant us courage,
    For the living of these days.

3. Cure thy children's warring madness,
   Bend our pride to thy control;
   Shame our wanton, selfish gladness,
   Rich in things and poor in soul.
   Grant us wisdom, grant us courage,
   Lest we miss thy kingdom's goal.

4. Set our feet on lofty places;
   Gird our lives that they may be
   Armoured with all Christ-like graces
   In the fight to set men free.
   Grant us wisdom, grant us courage,
   That we fail not man nor thee.
   Amen.

67. God, make us your family

Tim Whipple

Refrain
Your kingdom come, your will be done,
   Now that we have become your sons.
Let the prayer of our hearts daily be:
   God, make us your family.

1. The eyes of the blind shall be opened;
   The ears of the deaf shall hear.
   The chains of the lame will be broken;
   Streams will flow in deserts of fear.

2. The ransomed of the Lord shall return;
   The islands will sing his songs at last.
   The chaff from the wheat shall be burned;
   His kingdom on earth, it shall come to pass.

3. The nations will see their shame;
   The one true God will be adored.
   They'll turn from their fortune and fame;
   His holy mountain shall be restored.

Optional Refrain for Christmastide
Laude, lauda, laude, lauda,
   Gloria Emmanuel.
Laude, lauda, laude, lauda,
   Gloria Emmanuel.

68.   Once no people
Maggie Durran
Based on 1 Pet. 2:9-10

Refrain
For we are a chosen race,
   a royal priesthood, holy nation.
Once no people, now God's people,
   proclaiming his marvellous light.

1. Sing the songs of faithful Zion,
      We are the stars and the grains of sand.
   Through our faith we are made glorious;
      We are Sons of Abraham.

2. Dance the steps of joyful Zion,
      Cymbals, harps and tambourines.
   Blow the trumpet, sound the glory
      In the presence of the Lord.

3. Taste the fruit of peaceful valleys,
      Sip of the wine and eat the bread.
   Know the shepherd who is guiding,
      The Lord, the Lamb of God.

4. We will serve through tribulation,
   We will follow to the cross.
   Know the death and pain of suffering;
   God wipes the tears from our eyes.

69. Comfort ye

Clint Taylor

Refrain
Comfort ye, comfort ye, my people.
Thus saith the Lord.

1. Bear each other up in your times of trouble
   Strengthen yourselves in your times of peace.

2. Love one another as I have loved you,
   Everything else will fall into place.

3. Bless the Lord for his great mercy,
   Especially for his Son Jesus Christ.

4. By my Spirit you have great power
   Which enables you to do my work.

70. Wherever two or more

Brian Howard
Based on Matt. 18:20
1 John 1:7, 3:1

Refrain
Wherever two or more are gathered in my name,
   There I am, there I am;
Wherever two or more are gathered in my name,
   There I am in the midst of them.

1. Behold what manner of love the Father gives
   That we should be called the sons of God.
   And now little children, abide in the Lord;
   We shall all be like him.

2. If we walk in the light as he is in the light,
   We shall always live with him;
   For the blood of Jesus Christ
   Sets us free from sin.

71. In the name of Jesus

Anon.

In the name of Jesus, in the name of Jesus
   We have the victory.
In the name of Jesus, in the name of Jesus
   Demons will have to flee.
Who can tell what God can do?
Who can tell of his love for you?
In the name of Jesus, Jesus,
   We have the victory.

72. Fight the good fight

John S. B. Monsell

1. Fight the good fight with all thy might,
   Christ is thy strength and Christ thy right;
   Lay hold on life, and it shall be
   Thy joy and crown eternally.

2. Run the straight race through God's good grace,
   Lift up thine eyes and seek his face;
   Life with its way before us lies,
   Christ is the path and Christ the prize.

3. Cast care aside, lean on thy Guide,
His boundless mercy will provide;
Trust, and thy trusting soul shall prove
Christ is its life and Christ its love.

4. Faint not, nor fear, his arms are near;
He changeth not, and thou art dear;
Only believe, and thou shalt see
That Christ is all in all to thee.

73. Jesus is a-drivin' out Satan

Mary Ackroyd

1. Jesus is a-drivin' out Satan
From ev'rywhere under the sun.
Jesus is a-drivin' out Satan,
You'd better get up, Satan, and run.

Refrain
Jesus is the victor,
Jesus, God's son.
Jesus is the King,
The battle is won.

2. Jesus is a mighty warrior,
He teaches us how to fight.
"Take my shield and my helmet and my double-edged
sword."
Satan fades in the sight of the right.

3. He gives us his blood and body;
In his strength we must rest.
We aren't the ones who fight the battle
When Satan puts us to the test.

4. You win the battle for us,
        We claim the power you give.
    We are your lovin' people,
        And by your word we will live.

74.   Faith is the victory

Refrain: John Yates
Verses: Betty Pulkingham

1. If there's a mountain that needs to be moved,
    If there's an obstacle right in your way,
    Listen intently and God will speak to you.
    Trust and obey him, come what may.

Refrain
Faith is the victory.
Faith is the victory.
Oh glorious victory
That overcomes the world.

2. Sarah and Abraham trusted God truly,
    God promised them he would give them a son.
    Many years passed, they were getting no younger,
    Nothing's impossible, Isaac did come.

3. Three years and a half in the days of Elijah
    It did not rain, the famine was sore.
    Elijah prayed and a cloud appeared yonder;
    He thanked God and it started to pour!

4. In times of war Gideon looked after his safety,
    Shrinking behind the wine press was he.
    God sent his angel who spoke to him thusly:
    "You valiant and mighty man, God is with thee."

75. When I survey the wondrous cross

Isa

1. When I survey the wondrous cross
   On which the prince of glory died
   My richest gain I count but loss,
   And pour contempt on all my pride.

2. Forbid it, Lord, that I should boast
   Save in the cross of Christ my God;
   All the vain things that charm me most,
   I sacrifice them to his blood.

3. See from his head, his hands, his feet,
   Sorrow and love flow mingling down;
   Did e'er such love and sorrow meet,
   Or thorns compose so rich a crown?

4. Were the whole realm of nature mine,
   That were an off'ring far too small;
   Love so amazing, so divine,
   Demands my soul, my life, my all.

76.   I am persuaded

Joan Hettenhouser

I am persuaded that neither death, nor life,
   Nor angels nor principalities,
Nor powers, nor things present,
   Nor anything to come,
Nor height, nor depth,
   Nor any other creature
   Shall be able to separate us
From the love of God,
   Which is in Christ Jesus our Lord.

77.   ## On Jordan's stormy banks

Samuel Stennett

1. On Jordan's stormy banks I stand
    And cast a wishful eye
    To Canaan's fair and happy land
    Where my possessions lie.

Refrain
I am bound for the promised land,
  I am bound for the promised land.
O who will come and go with me
  I am bound for the promised land.

2. When shall I reach that happy place
    And be for ever blest?
    When shall I see my Father's face.
    And in his bosom rest?

78.   ## Come go with me to that land

Traditional

1. Well, come go with me to that land,
      Come go with me to that land,
    Come go with me to that land
      Where I'm bound.
    Come go with me to that land,
      Come go with me to that land,
    To that land, to that land,
      Where I'm bound.

2. There's gonna be lovin' in that land,
      Gonna be lovin' in that land,
    Gonna be lovin' in that land
      Where I'm bound.
    Gonna be lovin' in that land,
      Gonna be lovin' in that land,
    In that land, in that land,
      Where I'm bound.